Practical Pre-School Books

What does it mean to be four?

A practical guide to child development
in the Early Years Early Years Foundation Stage

Jennie Lindon

Contents

Published by Step Forward Publishing Limited
St Jude's Church, Dulwich Road, Herne Hill, London, SE24 0PB Tel. 020 7738 5454
Revised edition © Step Forward Publishing Limited 2008
First edition © Step Forward Publishing Limited 2006
www.practicalpreschoolbooks.com

What does it mean to be four? (Revised edition) ISBN: 978 1 904575 41 2

Focus on four-year-olds

What Does it Mean to be Four? explores the developmental needs and likely skills of four-year-olds. This book is complete in itself but fours develop along their own personal timeline. So the content links closely with the other three titles in this series, especially with *What does it mean to be three?* and *What does it mean to be five?* The content of this book is relevant to any practitioners, working with fours anywhere in the UK. The structure of the book, however, follows the framework for England of the Early Years Foundation Stage: guidance covering from birth to five years of age that will be statutory for early years provision from September 2008.

Each book in the *What does it mean to be...?* series recognises that many children from the age group will attend different kinds of early years provision, as well as being part of their own family home. Even children, whose family have chosen childminding, are very likely now to spend part of their week in some kind of group setting. Since a proportion of fours attend early years provision on school grounds, some of them also join a form of out-of-school provision, such as a breakfast club, after-school or holiday club. However, the objective in this book is to approach four-year-olds as individuals whose uniqueness should not be limited to their role in attending a given type of early years provision, nor by increasingly being seen by adults as a young 'school pupil'. Children's learning can only be effectively and appropriately supported when adults - practitioners and parents alike - are guided by sound knowledge of child development: what children are like at different ages and what they therefore need in order to thrive.

The layout of each of the four books in this linked series includes:

- Descriptive developmental information within the main text, organised within the six areas of learning used by the Early Years Foundation Stage.
- 'For example' sections giving instances of real children and real places and sometimes references to useful sources of further examples.
- 'Being a helpful adult' boxes which focus on adult behaviour that is an effective support for children's learning, as well as approaches that could undermine young children.
- 'Food for thought' headings which highlight points of good practice in ways that can encourage reflection and discussion among practitioners, as well as sharing in partnership with parents.

Where are the fours 'officially'?

Four-year-olds are welcome in any of the different types of early years provision: nursery schools and classes, reception classes, playgroups and pre-schools, day nurseries and different types of centres for young children and with the childminding service. Families are strongly encouraged nowadays to accept some kind of out-of-home early years experience for their four-year-olds, but across the UK attendance is mainly voluntary. However, a different national framework operates in each country of the UK:

- In England from September 2008 the three to five Foundation Stage early years curriculum, will be replaced by the birth to five years framework of the Early Years Foundation Stage. This framework, just like the Foundation Stage, applies until the end of the reception class, provision that is located within a primary school.

- In Scotland, the Curriculum Framework for Children 3-5 applies to the experiences of fours. Current developments focus on a Curriculum for Excellence to cover from three to eighteen years of age. In the earlier years, the main focus for development is for a continuity of more active learning and play from the early education of three to five years olds into the first years of primary school.
- In Wales, the main focus of development is on the Foundation Phase for young children from three to seven years, bridging the early years curriculum into the first years of primary school.
- In Northern Ireland the Curricular Guidance for Pre-School Education applies to three- and four-year-olds. However, in Northern Ireland young children start primary school in the September of the school year after their fourth birthday. So many fours are in primary school. The main focus for current development is the Foundation Stage that applies to the first two years of primary school, with children aged four or five years of age.

Development matters in the Early Years Foundation Stage (EYFS)

From September 2008 in England fours are 'officially' within a framework that spans the full range of early childhood. All early years practitioners in England need to become familiar with the details of the EYFS but the good practice described is not new. Part of your task, in finding your way around the EYFS materials, is recognising just how much is familiar when your early years provision already has good practice. (See page 64 for information on how to access materials about the EYFS.) The EYFS follows the pattern of developmental areas, established with the Foundation Stage, and there are only a few changes within the details of that structure.

There are six areas of learning within the EYFS.

- Personal, Social and Emotional Development
- Communication, Language and Literacy
- Problem Solving, Reasoning and Numeracy
- Knowledge and Understanding of the World
- Physical Development
- Creative Development

This framework is one way of considering the breadth of children's learning. But of course children do not learn in separate compartments; the whole point is that children's learning crosses all the boundaries. The aim of identifying areas of learning is to help adults to create a balance, to address all the different, equally important areas of what children gain across the years of early childhood.

When the EYFS is in place, all these records have to connect with the six areas of learning. A rich resource of developmental information and practice advice is provided in the Practice Guidance booklet of the EYFS, in Appendix 2 that runs from pages 22-114. None of this material should be used as a checklist, or have-to-do grids. It is crucial that early years practitioners and teams hold tight to this key point. In each of these very full pages, the same pattern applies.

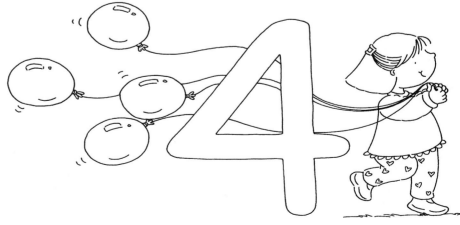

- The developmental information in the first column, 'Development matters', is a reminder of the kinds of changes likely to happen – not an exhaustive list of what happens, and in this exact way. The examples work like the Stepping Stones guidance of the Foundation Stage.
- The broad and overlapping age spans are deliberate: birth to 11 months, 8-20 months, 16-26 months, 22-36 months, 30-50 months and 40-60+ months. The aim is to refresh about development, supporting practitioners to take time over all the 'steps'. There should be no headlong rush to the final early learning goals (ELGs). None of the descriptions, apart from the ELGs, are required targets or outcomes.
- So, the only part of all this information that is statutory is the description of the early learning goals. They only become relevant for observation within the last year of the EYFS (just like with the Foundation Stage), which is the reception class located in primary schools.
- Practitioners working with younger fours will look initially within the 30-50 months span. This section of developmental information is also the most appropriate span if you work with children whose development has been significantly slowed by disability or very limited early experience. There should be no sense of rush, but the details of the 40-60+ age band will become more central.
- The ELGs, placed at the end of every 40-60+ age band, should not be used to shape the experiences of fours. It is appropriate for practitioners to be increasingly aware of how the older fours are progressing towards those goals. However, it is important to hold tight to the fact that the ELGs are set as expectations for most children to achieve by the end of the EYFS. The specific point, as defined on page 11 of the statutory guidance is 'by the end of the academic year in which they reach the age of five.'

Child-focussed observation and planning

It will be necessary for practitioners (in England) to adjust their flexible forward planning and child-focussed documentation to reflect the six areas of the EYFS from September 2008. However, the adjustments are minor for those practitioners who have already been working with the Foundation Stage framework. Practitioners with mixed age groups, including children of two, three and four years of age, can leave behind the frustrating problems of creating a bridge between the aspects and components structure of *Birth to Three Matters* and a framework of six developmental areas. Early years practitioners should have a sound basis of child development knowledge. If any practitioners feel unsure of realistic expectations, then the Development matters column should be used as a detailed source of information to build that knowledge across early childhood.

The situation about any kind of written planning and documentation is the same as has applied all the time for the Foundation Stage, namely that there are no statutory written formats for observation and planning. The early years inspection body for England, Ofsted, does not require any specific approach to the need to be observant and to have a planful approach. The EYFS materials offer suggestions, including the flexible approach of the Learning Journey, which is described on the CD ROM materials linked with the Principles into Practice card '3.1. Observation, assessment and planning.' But no format is compulsory. The key messages from the EYFS materials are that any formats used by practitioners need to show:

- The progress of individual children over time, at their own pace and set against realistic expectations for their age, ability and experiences.
- That planning is responsive to the needs and interests of individual children: through continuous provision in the learning environment and flexible use of planned activities.

- How observations of children make a difference to what is offered to individuals and to sensible short-term changes to planning opportunities for a group of children.
- There is plenty of scope for fine-tuning through short-term planning – that 'what next?' or 'next steps' are a real part of the process.

Over the same pages 22-114 of the EYFS Practice Guidance each page has other information and suggestions:

- Look, listen and note (second column in from the left) is a resource of suggestions, very like the 'examples of what children do' in the Foundation Stage. This is not a list of the observations everyone has to do; they are reminders of the pitch and level at which it makes sense to observe across that age range.
- The other two columns - 'Effective practice' and 'Planning and resourcing' - are similar to the right hand pages throughout the Foundation Stage file entitled 'what does the practitioner need to do?'

Young children – not school pupils

Of course fours have been busy learning already. Based on positive early experiences they will have learned a great deal at home with their families, during their time with childminders and in early years settings that offer childcare for children as young as babies. Across the UK it is increasingly likely that most children will now experience some kind of group provision. In Northern Ireland, the fours will enter primary school. But children continue to learn in the home situation, whether with their own family or, for the many children who continue with their childminder, in another family home. Partnership with parents continues to be crucial. It is just as important for practitioners to understand how children learn at home as for parents to share in the aims and experiences of their child's early years setting.

The aim of the Early Years Foundation Stage is to create a coherent pattern over the years of early childhood. But this laudable objective faces an early years system full of changes for children. It is not unusual that young children are moved by their parents from a nursery or centre, that still welcomes the fours, to a nursery class based in a primary school. Of course, good nursery class provision will benefit children, but some parents seem doubtful that early learning can take place in any setting outside school grounds. Some schools also put pressure on parents to take up a nursery place, let alone reception, on the grounds (possibly true in some cases) that there may not be a spare place later.

Fours need help to cope with these changes and practitioners need to work together to ensure a proper transition. Part of this kind of partnership has to be that the team in the next setting respect and take notice of the observational records developed by the team who has come to know this four-year-old as a unique young child.

In England, it proved a tough task for some reception teams to hold tight to the Foundation Stage guidance in reception class on school grounds. Primary schools vary and some heads have been very committed to working from the youngest upwards rather than imposing a top-down educational strategy. However, strong pressure has undoubtedly been exerted on some reception teams to get children ready for Key Stage One. Year One teachers experience their own pressures and adult anxiety has sometimes rolled down the age bands to teams working with fours and sometimes even with three-year-olds in some nursery classes.

Supportive early years practitioners need to focus on what are the priorities for four-year-olds rather than the demands, which are sometimes disruptive and unrealistic, that steamroller down from an older age band. Fours can be seriously lost in a system that wants to define them in terms of specific achievements that are required later in the school years. A tyranny can develop that undermines four-year-old learning when they are regarded firmly through a 'pre-school' lense. The children's accomplishments can then be defined as important only in so far as they are more ready for later tasks.

The very strong focus on child development in the EYFS has to be used to challenge views that earlier must be better in the establishment of skills. The same focus needs to challenge that some aspects of learning, such as the cognitive skills, are more important, or that physical or emotional development are optional extras, if there is time in a busy session or day. When practitioners lose sight of realistic expectations, this confusion is often linked with an unbalanced view of the areas of child development.

The focus in this book is on four-year-olds in their own right and within the continued flow of their own development. It is very important that early years practitioners start with the children themselves. There are high risks in starting with a framework for four-year-olds that is determined by their role as 'pupils' and the demands of school, and then young children are pushed to fit. Sensitive adults, practitioners and parents, are aware of the need to help children prepare for school life. But the children's skills, interests and knowledge should not be judged as only valuable insofar as they support the children to take on the role of 'school pupil'.

What makes a helpful adult?

Some of the confusion about how best to support the learning of young children seems to arise from an image of school learning and the behaviour of school teachers.

The Early Years Foundation Stage guidance uses the term 'practitioner' to refer to all adults involved in supporting children's learning. It is useful that the words 'teach' and 'teaching' (prominent in the Foundation Stage) have been replaced. There is a very strong emphasis on play as the most powerful, and appropriate, vehicle for early learning. However, the phrase 'educational programmes' has been chosen to describe the framework of experiences. These words continue to carry a weight that may still create some difficulties in practice. The wording in the EYFS also focuses on the importance of 'planned and purposeful' play. This broad concept has caused some problems over the years, when adults become over-keen on their plans and purposes.

Some early years practitioners, and parents as well, appear to have linked 'early education' and discussion about 'educational goals' with their childhood memories of school, school work and teachers. But these memories are from a time later in childhood than the EYFS, even if they are accurate memories. Uneasy early years practitioners, especially without specific guidance from managers, have concluded that to support early learning they must behave close to their selective memories of what a 'teacher' does. This model has included greater adult direction of children's activities, including excessive use of paper and pencil activities through worksheets. There has sometimes been too strong a focus on group activities, rather than individual exploration and interests. In short, anxious practitioners, with the best of intentions, have sometimes created more of a classroom feel, even for very young children. The balance between adult-initiated and child-initiated activities has tipped too much towards adult direction.

Yet, of course, good nursery teachers do not behave at all the same way as teachers of primary school age children. Effective early years practitioners of a non-teaching background need to step away from the 'school teacher' model in their mind. Good nursery teachers have long followed the threads of children's current thinking and created a welcoming environment that enables children to learn through play and nursery routines.

Several research projects in recent years have worked to identify the most effective approaches to supporting the learning of young children, often called pedagogy, which includes the behaviour of early years and school practitioners and the details of the learning environment that they help to create and maintain. The project on Researching Effective Pedagogy in the Early Years (part of the EPPE project) has been led by Iram Siraj-Blatchford. This team made detailed observations in early years settings identified as having good practice from the main EPPE project. Several practical issues emerged through their findings:

- Good learning outcomes for children are linked to adult-child interactions that involve what the team called 'sustained shared thinking' and open-ended questioning to extend children's thinking (see the example on page 44)
- Practitioners need a thorough knowledge of the early years curriculum framework, but grounded in sound knowledge and understanding of child development.
- Educational aims need to be shared with parents. In some settings the team judged that parents were engaging in as much, if not more, sustained shared thinking with their children than the practitioners undertook within the setting.
- Children benefit from constructive feedback from adults during activities: a few comments about what had gone well, suggestions or connections with what a child has already learned.
- Teams need to establish a positive approach to behaviour, through a behaviour policy and adult practice that values problem-solving. Such an outlook supported good learning outcomes for children, since they learn to be assertive and to use language to talk through conflicts.

The most effective settings provided a balance between adult-initiated activities and play activities freely chosen by the children, but from a learning environment and materials that had potential for learning. According to the team the best balance for early learning was about two-thirds child-initiated to one-third adult-initiated experiences. But the whole point was that alert practitioners were ready to come alongside children in their freely chosen enterprises. Helpful adults added a comment and joined in the play and conversation, without taking over the control. Supportive adult-initiated experiences were not utterly controlled by the adults: an engaging activity was started but then children had a lot of influence over what happened next. The team observed that even in good reception classes, it was far more likely that the balance tipped much more towards adult-initiated activities and many of these were run in small groups. This issue is revisited in *What does it mean to be five?*.

Early years practitioners who were trained teachers were observed to undertake the most effective interactions with children, with greater amounts of sustained shared thinking. Non-teacher trained practitioners were most effective when working under the guidance of trained teachers. The possible dynamic here, although not one described specifically in the report, is that the teacher-trained practitioners were able to show colleagues not only a supportive style of interaction, but also showed by example how 'teachers' behave with younger children.

Personal, Social and Emotional Development

Four-year-olds are still young children. We need to remember that these boys and girls are the same children as the three-year-olds discussed in *What Does it Mean to be Three?* They are just a little older, with some more knowledge and skills and perhaps some confusions and self-doubts. In a supportive early years setting, with adults who tune in to how four-year-olds think, children continue to develop a positive sense of themselves, as individuals who are liked and appreciated. They can be building a positive and realistic sense of self-esteem.

For example

Many of this age group will still need the reassurance of a special toy or cuddly. Supportive early years practitioners respect this wish for a very young child to have a physical and emotional connection with home. Any early years setting, like a childminder's home, should have a safe personal space for each child - a basket or drawer – where important items can be placed, when they no longer need to be held. Some settings take trouble to gather photos from home, given by parents, often laminate them for longer life, and ensure that children can easily look at a photo of Mummy, the new baby, the family pet – again any connection that helps to bridge the gap.

Sometimes parents are more concerned that they need to be. For instance, one of the many valuable observations described by Jacqui Cousins (*Listening to Four Year Olds*) was her realisation that a reception class team was fully accepting of children's cuddlies. It was the parents who had gained the wrong idea that cuddlies were not allowed. The staff had asked that children did not bring in their own toys, expect on special occasions. However, cuddlies were an understood exception and were respected despite the tatty state of some much loved teddies or little blankets.

Personal and social awareness

Four-year-olds can be enthusiastic about learning and their capacity to continue to learn. But this outlook is closely linked with their experience, and with their personal, social and emotional well-being. Children will always learn from their experience, it is just that they do not always take away in their young minds what unreflective adults assume or intended that they would learn.

In over-directed and harassed early years settings, children learn that adults require you to 'do your work', that chatting is an interruption of proper concentration or that it is right and proper to fret about your capabilities as a four-year-old. (See the examples on page 40 and the 'Food for thought' box). In more relaxed settings, adults feel more confident to let children learn. There, four-year-olds, and their younger or older companions, know that they can take their time to complete a project to their own satisfaction, that adults are interested in their views or that they are a valued member of the setting. (See pages 14 and 38).

Four-year-olds can be well able to pay attention, using their skills of looking and listening. The task for helpful adults is to keep a flexible outlook on what is meant by attention and concentration, based on realistic expectations for children who are still very young. Children of this age still find it hard to keep still, especially when sitting in a group with other children whose knees and elbows are very close. They also find it hard to wait to share something of interest out loud and enthusiastic children can risk being labelled as 'interrupters' and 'lacking patience' when they are more accurately described as 'keen communicators'.

Four-year-olds generally are happy to be closer to other people than adults choose. But this does not apply all the time and to everyone. Four-year-olds move in very close, to easy touching distance, when they are keen to communicate, feel happy with the adult or child or want to get a closer look at something of interest. Four-year-olds do not want to be close to every child, nor to be trapped in a confined space with somebody who pokes them or whispers irritating remarks.

It is difficult to explain why some practitioners expect children to sit still on carpet, which often feels uncomfortable after a short period of time. Children manage this tough task when their minds are engaged in an interesting activity and they are allowed some degree of movement. The same adults would almost certainly not be able to stay still even on chairs with the level of distraction that develops in some group carpet times!

For example

In New River Green a mixed group of three- and four-year-olds were able to watch and wait in a friendly atmosphere with interest and the chance to chat. They were waiting their turn to be involved in a hand painting activity offered on the outdoor veranda.

One practitioner and an older child, present for the summer holidays, were doing designs on the back of children's hands if they wished. The children were able to choose from several possible designs and then pick the colours they wanted.

The two children being painted at any one time were able to stay still while the design was painted. The surrounding small group of three- and four-year-olds was also able to be patient. They watched intently as the designs were painted, talked about what design they might want when it was their turn and pointed to the colours in the unusual little pots. They were also interested to quiz the older child to whom the materials belonged. One child wanted to know, 'is that your own brush from home?'

(See page 68 for details of people and places mentioned in examples).

Four-year-olds are more able to manage the social interaction that goes on in a small group but they are still young and need to feel they are getting personal interaction. Large groups are hard for them and it is unwise for nurseries or playgroups to try to have interactive group times with more than 20 three- and four-year-olds. Even the most experienced of early years practitioners can find it hard going to engage everyone. Less experienced or fraught practitioners can find themselves getting increasingly annoyed with the children who find it most difficult to sit still.

For example

Four-year-olds enjoy and learn from domestic routines. They can be part of sociable mealtimes in full day facilities and when they move to a full day in sessional nurseries. Fours can manage some

Being a helpful adult

It is important for early years practitioners to communicate with parents about what their children are learning and how. Displays, conversations and open evenings or sessions reassure parents that their four-year-olds are progressing in their development and show how early literacy and numeracy, in particular, build up in early childhood.

Unless parents have professional experience of the early years, they will tend to assume that 'proper learning' is close to their memories of primary school. Most parents are pleased to hear how their young children are developing skills in literacy and numeracy. Through friendly discussions you can also highlight what they are doing at home with their children to support this learning.

time within small groups. One of those opportunities is their willingness to enjoy snack and meal times. They also learn a great deal by happy involvement in domestic routines.

In New River Green children have lunch on tables that sit up to eight. I joined a group that was spread between two tables. One of the tables was known by the children as 'the sensible table' because it did not have an adult sitting at the table and children were chosen each day as able to be trusted. The early years practitioner was close by on the second table in the same area and there was no sense whatsoever of not being a sensible child if you sat at that table. It was much more that everyone got a chance to sit at the children-only table and three- and four-year-olds sounded proud as they came across from washing their hands and announced, 'I'm on the sensible table today'.

- All the children (three-, four- and a few five-year-olds because it was summer holiday time) dished up for themselves from open dishes. They all waited until everyone had dished up what they wanted. The two table groups were patient, asking from time to time, 'Can we start now?' but accepting the explanation from the practitioner of, 'not yet, everybody hasn't got their food.'
- One child per table took the beakers with drink around to each child and set them on the table. The two children took great care and there was a relaxed feel to the mealtime.
- While they were waiting to start, some three- and four-year-olds started spontaneously - the practitioner did not make the suggestion - to count up how many children there were at their table. Rosie (three years old) could count the children accurately by pointing as she said each number. She got the total correct, except that she did not count herself - quite a common mistake with younger children. Chris and Harry (both four-year-olds) were less confident about the counting. They knew some numbers but seemed slightly confused between finger counting and looking at each child in turn and pointing. The boys did not reach an accurate total in the end but seemed enthusiastic about the trying.
- Dessert was tinned peach slices and some fresh fruit. The practitioner was careful about sharing out the slices and the children watched closely. A friendly discussion ensued about how many slices were possible. One child asked, 'I want three' and the practitioner explained, 'we'll have to see how many there are. I'm sharing them out.' Once she had gone round all the children who wanted peaches, the practitioner commented, 'now I'll have some peaches. You've all got three. So there's some left for me.'
- A bit later one child perked up with, 'We haven't had seconds' and the practitioner explained patiently, 'there wasn't enough for seconds. They've all gone. Nobody's had seconds. It's not just you.' The child followed up with 'why?' and the explanation was given, 'because there was not a lot of peaches today'. The child repeated back, 'cos there was not a lot of peaches today.' The whole conversation was calm and there was no sense of complaint. The exchange was a timely reminder that fair shares of peach slices is important when you are four years old.

Friendly relations with peers and adults

Close friendships can develop between four-year-old boys and girls whose early years setting is organised in ways that enable and encourage social contact. Adults often acknowledge in words, spoken or written, that children's social development is important. Yet daily practice in some settings does not always reflect this value to the full.

Children need relaxed social contact for them to learn that their peers have a different viewpoint on an event or a priority. Some social learning can develop through well handled small group discussion, for instance in circle time or arising from children's spontaneous comments about stories or puppet play. But four-year-olds want and need to relate such activities closely to their own personal experience (see the example about Persona dolls on page 20).

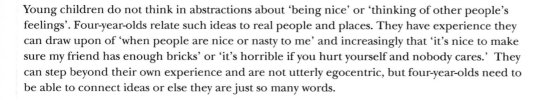

Young children do not think in abstractions about 'being nice' or 'thinking of other people's feelings'. Four-year-olds relate such ideas to real people and places. They have experience they can draw upon of 'when people are nice or nasty to me' and increasingly that 'it's nice to make sure my friend has enough bricks' or 'it's horrible if you hurt yourself and nobody cares.' They can step beyond their own experience and are not utterly egocentric, but four-year-olds need to be able to connect ideas or else they are just so many words.

For example

Children value friendships and, when asked what they like about nursery or the early years of primary school, three-, four- and five-year-olds often emphasise the importance of friends.

Children value friendships and, when asked what they like about nursery or the early years of primary school, threes to fives frequently emphasise the importance of friends. Consultation projects with young children often find that they focus on the importance of having a friend – sometimes through the questioning technique of 'what will Teddy like about nursery?' Older fours and then fives are often able to say that they, or children in general, are unhappy when they are temporarily without friends or they cannot get to join in the play of other children.

Fours often act on this understanding in a prosocial and empathetic way. My son's first week at nursery class, as a nearly four, was made easier because he and another boy of the same age started on the same day. Drew and Matthew locked together to keep each other company: a friendship that lasted until they went to different secondary schools. My own daughter's first week at nursery, as a three-year-old, was eased by two four-year-olds, both of them boys and only one child was already known to her. Henry and Tom chose to keep Tanith close company, explaining how everything worked through the session and making sure she was not sad.

Four-year-olds, even those without siblings at home, are often caring towards the younger children, and in settings with a full early years age range are keen to be part of the caring routines. Some four-year-olds use their pretend play to explore the practical ideas of baby care and what it means to be much younger. But their understanding is effectively supported by real contact across the age ranges when a setting offers this opportunity.

- Older children enjoy communicating with babies and toddlers. The four-year-olds gain pleasure from making younger ones laugh and are often good at the repetitive 'do it again' games that under-twos adore.
- They show an impressive understanding of communication (and a lack of egocentricity) when they adjust their style of communication for babies or young toddlers. Four-year-olds who have contact with much younger children know, for example, that simpler words and sentence construction is necessary.
- In early years settings, as well as family homes, four-year-olds often choose to 'read' a book to a younger child or to join in shared games that enable the younger child to have a clear role.
- Four-year-olds can become irritated with younger children, siblings or not, if adults allow a situation in which the slightly older children can rarely get any peace. But the times when social games become squabbling should not detract from the social skills that four-year-olds show at other times.

Food for thought

- Children need, by and large, to be able to choose their own friends. It is appropriate that early years practitioners are observant to ensure that children do not reject each other on the basis of their sex, ethnic group or disability. But attempts by adults to make children be friends risk backfiring.
- In a friendly atmosphere where adults discreetly oil the social wheels, young children build friendships across any boundaries of grouping: age, social, ethnic or religious groups, language differences and across disability.
- However, children may find it hard to sustain friendly relations when they cannot find shared ground. They are not necessarily being actively unfriendly, but a continued lack of a shared language may complicate play that depends on spoken communication, such as role play.
- Children whose disabilities make it hard for them to understand play (for instance children with autistic spectrum disorder) may not be easy play companions and adults need to keep fair and realistic expectations of other four-year-olds in the group.

Food for thought

Recent developments for childcare, included extended school day provision, has been driven mainly by the demands of the workplace and by the resulting needs of parents.

A lot of childcare provision that has developed recently, and wrap-around care for school age children, has been driven by the demands of the workplace and by the needs - and choices - of parents, who have to handle varied work or study patterns and keep their childcare costs within a budget. But the consequences for young children can be disruptive of their social networks and ability to understand how their day will work.

Highly flexible patterns of attendance at nursery or pre-school are not positive experiences for four-year-olds, who may become familiar with the practitioners but cannot make friends because they do not meet the same children on a predictable basis. Complex childcare arrangements running across each day can also require children as young as four years (many of whom are in school Reception classes) to handle several separate transitions within a single day.

Even if each setting and adult(s) are friendly and welcoming, four-year-olds have to negotiate a high level of change of context, with different adult expectations and ground rules. Most adults would object to an equivalent amount of daily movement within their working life.

The importance of touch and friendly physical contact is raised in the books in this series about two- and three-year-olds. But of course the need for friendly communication through touch extends throughout early childhood. Fours, just like their younger selves, need to feel emotionally safe and at ease with their important adults in out-of-home provision. Perhaps fours will not need a reassuring cuddle very often. But a child who is unhappy for some reason or who has fallen over, will feel rejected if there is no prospect of reassurance and comfort from touch. Fours still often want to say 'hello, I'm back!' with a full body hug or the cuddle that says, 'haven't we done brilliantly!' They want to get your attention by touch and accept that you do that as well.

Restrictions on this kind of important human contact in early years provision have become entangled in some settings with a serious misunderstanding about good safeguarding practice. Practitioners have been made anxious about the risk of allegations of sexual abuse and sometimes about the consequences of using adult strength wisely to keep young children safe from hurting themselves and others. This problem of 'adult protection' seems to be especially fraught in some schools and so affects provision, not only reception class, located on school grounds.

Readers who face this practice dilemma will need to seek further advice around genuinely protective practice with children. I explore the concerns and the best practice decisions in detail in my *Safeguarding Children and Young People* and more briefly in *Care and Caring* (see page 66). The main point is that all early years practitioners must focus on the 'child' in 'child protection'. There are no national requirements – arising from child protection guidance or any other framework - that demand practitioners follow no-touch regimes, that will inevitably undermine children's personal and social development. Nor is there any support for an adult reluctance to meet four-year-olds' continuing need for occasional help in their personal care, for instance over toileting accidents.

Social skills

Four-year-olds who have had supportive adults can be adept in many familiar social situations. However, they appreciate adult help when a situation has become too complex or emotionally heated for them to resolve. Four-year-olds tend to be able to:

- Approach an existing group of playing children and join them in a way that does not bring rejection by words or actions. Sometimes there is no way to join a closed friendship group and children on the outside need adult help to find playmates.
- Initiate and lead in a group or pairs situation. Four- and three-year-olds who are at ease with each other often develop long sequences in which the lead passes between individuals in a small group of children.
- Leave play and move on, although not always with ease, since some children face the difficulty of wanting a break from a peer who wishes to be their friend.
- Part of four-year-olds' social skills can be having the confidence to ask for help from an adult when play has become complicated or a conflict has developed that is beyond their skills to resolve. Much will then depend on the level of skill that adults show - see page 15. However, four-year-olds will vary and some children will bring experience and expectations into your setting that increase rather than reduce conflict.

Four-year-olds are able to anticipate to an extent the consequences of their actions and sometimes try to put matters right. Children learn by courteous adult reminders and explanations (see the practical examples on page 51).

Part of four-year-old social skills extend to how you can handle the situation when matters have gone awry. There are ways to show sorry that can be just as effective and genuine as saying the word and it is unwise to insist that only saying sorry is real evidence of regret. In a few settings that I have known, the emphasis on actually saying the word 'sorry' has degenerated into adult nagging. An atmosphere can be created in which four-year-olds, and younger children, are at risk of learning to use this particular magic word just to make adults go away. In a similar way, there are more ways to communicate appreciation and thanks than saying the actual words 'thank you'.

Making choices and accessing materials

Four-year-olds who are confident in your setting will manage a great deal on their own in terms of making choices and handling daily routines. Children experience personal satisfaction when they have a genuine part to play in domestic routines. They are far happier to get busy with the tidying or to be trusted to lay the table than to sit around waiting or tolerate a large group session while an adult does this work 'because it's quicker'.

Good early years teams look at the established pattern for daily routines. You can use your observation skills to explore whether there are times and locations within your setting that stretch four-year-old social skills and patience to breaking point. The best first option is to consider ways to change the situation so that you engage children and reduce tedious waiting time. The immediate idea that there must be something wrong with the children's behaviour is unhelpful, loses options for learning and, as the children would say, can be 'very unfair!'

For example

I have seen many examples of good practice in early years settings that enable three- and four-year-olds to make genuine choices, run their own routines to an extent and learn the skills of self-direction. The responsibility of adults is to organise the environment in ways that children can exercise choice and then to be available with help if children want it. Four-year-olds cannot develop as independent learners unless their learning environment is organised in ways that offer them choices.

In visits to different early years settings, I have seen teams, working in spaces of different size and shape, organise the environment to create the workshop or learning spaces approach.

- At the time that I visited it, St Peter's nursery class was located in the crypt (they have since moved to the main school site). But the team had creatively used all the spaces, large window seats and cubby holes, to provide areas in which play materials were gathered. Children themselves made many of the choices about what would be brought out each day.
- The nursery school that is part of Windham Early Excellence Centre has a large indoor space that the team deliberately reorganised into simpler workshop spaces: a construction area, writing/literacy area and a creative area. Materials for all the areas are stored in low shelving and other storage systems that are easily accessible to children. The team has forward planning, but has taken the approach of having less materials out on the tables or floors ready for children than they did previously. The reorganisation has meant that there is much more opportunity for children to get out what they want. (See also page 59.)
- When I visited Burnwood Nursery School, they had used furniture and other equipment to create enclosed spaces within the large nursery room. They had moved away from the home corner to a more flexible role-play concept that could be responsive to children's interests. At that time they had a hairdressers' shop and post office. The nursery had a book corner but had made the decision to get some books out into the other learning spaces as well. There were art books close by the creative/painting area and books about construction close to the building materials. This informal distribution gave young children the strong message that books were for them to consult and were useful in many ways, not just for enjoyment at story time.
- Burnwood Nursery School, like a number of other settings I have visited, had a simple and effective system of self-registration and avoided the milling around and waiting that can be created by the more traditional method. Each child had a pair of large cards, one to find on a table and then match to its pair on a standing display. In the three-year-olds' room the cards had a photo and the child's first name. In the four-year-olds' room their card had no photo and their full name, since these children were now adept at the procedure.
- The Grove Nursery School team had reflected on the whole business of movement of materials between learning spaces. They agreed that writing materials should not have to stay in the writing/graphics area, so they had considered practical issues such as how writing materials, and other useful items, could also be in small carrying containers. Children were able to take materials to where they were working or to support their pretend play.

Consultation projects often find that threes and fours are very able to make genuine choices and be active decision makers within their early years setting. The Save the Children project, led by Lina Farjerman, offers many examples that demonstrate very clearly that children are able to develop their own projects. They benefit from adult help as needed, rather than always have adult-initiated and adult-led activities dominate their week. Working at their own pace, children are competent, and keen, to undertake their own documentation – with generous supplies of stationery and often a camera as well.

Young children are also more competent that adults often think – in terms of routine and less routine events. The Save the Children consultation resource gives the example of the three- and four-year-olds from the Hillside Nursery in Hackney, London. These children were actively involved by the staff in their own move from one room in the building to another. These young boys and girls were busy, with their familiar practitioners, in moving and then re-organising all their play resources and equipment. At the beginning of the next week, the children walked into the 'new' room that they had helped to organise.

Inviting children's views

You can read reports of some carefully considered and practical consultation projects with children aged from three to five years. See page 65 for details of projects. It is important that early years practitioners, and any other adults who wish to develop consultation with young children, are aware of a positive framework for consultation.

- You need to be clear about what you want to ask children. If you are vague about questions and issues, then children's answers will be vague or confused, too. It helps everyone to know that you would welcome ideas about how to reorganise the book corner or how to make the visit to the museum as enjoyable as possible.
- Adults need to consult on topics and situations over which the children can exercise genuine choice. Even young children soon work out that, 'they ask us but they don't listen to what we say'. Discussion and consultation must be genuine; avoid the temptation to get children to agree to, and rubber stamp, what you wanted to do in the first place.
- Adults show respect to children by being honest about decisions that have already been made by the adults. You can explain simply the reasoning behind the decision.
- Children can only generate ideas from what they know already. So it is not surprising if, given a very open brief, they tend to say they would like more, or less, of activities, food or anything with which they are already familiar. Adults need to create a balance between offering possibilities that may not strike young children and acting in ways that direct children's responses.

Abstract ideas can be puzzling for children when they do not easily connect with their experience so far. Early years settings have successfully used visual materials to bring options and opinions alive to three- to five-year-olds. Photos, drawings, magazine images and real items help children to understand the ideas. Opinions can be expressed with smiley/grumpy stickers or faces on a stick.

- You and the children need to find ways to record their views. Documentation can be visual as well as written. Adults may do the actual writing but children need to do much of the dictation.
- Adults need to consider what the children have said and how their views will visibly affect daily practice or the shape of a special event. Children need to hear and see how their views have been acted upon.
- When children have expressed preferences, they may sometimes question why someone else's choice was picked rather than their own. With support, and ensuring that there is overall fairness, young children steadily understand that this fact is part of group life.
- Children, who feel their views are welcomed, can be acute observers of the life of an early years setting. Sometimes their opinions may surprise or unsettle teams. Responsible adults need to reflect on what they have heard and not safeguard their level of comfort by interpreting children's honest responses as 'thoughtless' or 'rude.

Skills of social problem solving

The Early Years Foundation Stage guidance, just like all early years curriculum guidance across the UK, places a very strong emphasis on supporting children's personal, social and emotional development. There are many examples of a focus on the need for practitioners to act as positive role models through what they say and do. Indeed most of the early learning goals in PSED benefit from adult reflection along the lines of 'how do I set a good example of this goal in action through my own behaviour?' Four-year-olds listen and they look at adult actions and reactions. This generation of young children is no more impressed than previous ones with an adult philosophy of 'do as I say not as I do!'

The practical steps in conflict resolution with children are very similar to the skills using in adult problem solving and mediation. In order to help children to learn these skills, adults need to be aware of their approach to dealing with conflict. Some early years practitioners may need to reflect on their own attitudes towards disagreement, as well as their first reactions to hearing and seeing a conflict between children.

- Some practitioners have learned an approach of trying to distract children or to downplay the importance of what has clearly annoyed these boys and girls. Once the emotional temperature has rocketed, the problem will not be resolved by hopeful adult intervention along the lines of, 'does it really matter?' (clearly it does) or 'let's be nice to each other' (no chance of that now).
- Some practitioners say that they have no time, or 'in an ideal world' would try to help children learn appropriate skills. The implication is that, until utopia arrives, the adult will continue to decide who had a play item first and impose a solution on children.

The serious drawback of either approach is that firstly, the problem absorbing the children does not go away, and secondly the adult loses a valuable opportunity for children to learn to resolve similar situations in the future.

The REPEY project (see also page 7) noted differences between early years setting on this area of learning. Teams, in settings with considered and strong behaviour policies, were more effective in supporting children to talk through conflicts. The pattern seems likely to be that the adults had sorted out the options in their own mind and valued the time assigned to helping children learn skills in this way. Settings can be less effective when there is limited adult understanding and commitment to the skills of problem solving and conflict resolution. Adults need to be clear about what assertiveness looks like, and how it can be supported, in the four-year-old age group.

This approach requires that:

- Adults give the time to listen and enable children to talk, rather than deciding as an adult who is in the right or wrong, or who 'started it'.
- The time you give will not be lengthy and the benefits are that children are far more likely to calm down and to find a way to resolve the situation.
- Practitioners whose reaction is 'we don't have time for this; we've got too many other things to do!' need to consider what happens with children's learning if some time is not assigned in this way.
- You go across to children rather than call from a distance. Adult non-verbal behaviour helps children to calm down. When you speak quietly and move to be at eye level with children, the effect is far more calming in reality than calling or shouting at children to 'calm down!'

- Children are part of the solution and then learn skills that increasingly they will be able to apply without adult help in the less fraught situations. In settings that use this model, or a pattern very close to it, four and even three-year-olds visibly learn to negotiate some of the more low key daily conflicts. They learn the habit of talking rather than shouting and of listening rather than grabbing - at least some of the time.

High/Scope UK offers the most practical resources in which the skills of conflict resolution are shown to and shared with young children. (See page 67 for details.) In brief, this practical approach brings a calm adult presence, ensuring that children do not hurt each other. Adults step aside from 'who had it first' – you often have no idea – and focus on acknowledging children's feelings and helping them to let you know 'what has happened?'. There is a strong sense of 'what's the problem here?' and not 'who is causing the problem here?' Adults have to be, and be seen to be, fair and willing to let each child in a conflict be heard. Adults use their words to help children to use their own words and restate the problem in simple terms. Children are usually much calmer by now and able to take part in finding a way out of this current problem. Threes and fours, who have experienced this approach over time, are ready to contribute their own ideas. An adult talks with, not at, the children so they reach a workable solution together. An adult may offer an idea but does not impose.

Sharing in their own care and routines

Growing competence in self-care remains important for four-year-olds. Children feel more positive about themselves when they are able to carry out many of the tasks of dressing, eating and toileting, and to have respectful help when they need it. Many four-year-olds are able to deal with most of their undressing, dressing, simple personal hygiene, going to the toilet and daily tasks of organising themselves. Four-year-olds sometimes struggle with the harder clothes' fastenings and skills may become shaky when children are under heavy time pressure.

For example

During my visit to St Peter's nursery class I saw how the adults in this team actively value the caring side and promote a manageable independence. This was reflected in the children's behaviour.

- At mid-session drink time there were written name labels put onto mugs by one adult and today's child helper. The children identified their mug by the name. It was striking how the young three-year-olds were confident to ask the older nursery children (only four years) if they had picked the correct mug. I observed one young child with a mug approach an older girl who was busy at the writing table. The three-year-old asked, 'is this my name?' The older girl stopped her writing, looked happy to check and said warmly to the younger girl, 'yes. Well done!'
- The nursery involves children actively in the tidying-up routine, allowing time and help if needed for this part of the session. The large foam wedges needed to be stacked in one corner on shelving. The nursery had worked on a set of photos that showed several ways in which it was possible to stack the blocks. The boys who were busy in this corner were keen to show me the illustrations and explain that the photos were needed because the blocks were a tight fit. There was a moment when everything looked chaotic, but the nursery head commented in a low key way about how the task was going and the boys got back on track.

Food for thought

- Sometimes competent four-year-olds just need a helping hand or feel like being cosseted. It is important that adults do not become sharp with children along the lines of, 'you're perfectly capable of doing that yourself' or judgmental on age grounds: 'you're four years old, you ought to be able to…'
- Children are expected to be helpful in early years settings and this expectation is fair and positive. Adults ask children to do tasks, which those adults are perfectly capable of doing for themselves. Adults would be shocked if a child countered with, 'you're 28 years old, can't you put a tissue in the waste bin yet!' So early years practitioners need to consider the balance between independent self-care and a friendly, helpful atmosphere, and this is exactly how good teams behave.

Four-year-olds can be competent in the toilet but there will be some times when children inadvertently wet themselves. It matters a very great deal how these accidents are handled by adults. A sensitive approach can help a child to feel better; an unkind approach can make a child feel foolish and dirty. Individual children vary a great deal, as I observed during my visit to St Peter's nursery class.

- One girl was distressed at her accident and was immediately comforted by the practitioner who was with her outdoors. Nobody was even slightly cross. The child calmed and went to change her clothes accompanied by another practitioner. A short while later, the girl became upset once more and this second team member was just as supportive, halted in her help with changing and focused on the child, to reassure her that nobody was cross, that these things happen.
- A second child was positively chirpy about her accident. She told me (a visitor), 'I've wet myself a bit' and I asked if she wanted any help. She said she was fine and confidently sorted out dry clothes from the chest of drawers that children could easily access. She put her damp clothes in the hanging bag for washing. This girl took her time and nobody asked her to hurry up. At one point, in mid-change, she joined a group briefly and then had a chat with a practitioner to explain that she could not find a pair of trousers but thought these leggings would suit.

Four-year-olds are learning about emotions

Four-year-olds have made progress in learning about their own emotions and have some understanding that other people, adults as well as children, have feelings too. Much depends on children's experience so far and some four-year-olds will be able to express their feelings in words as well as the body language that communicates happiness, excitement, distress or frustration.

For example

In *Bad Guys don't have Birthdays: Fantasy Play at Four* (Chicago University Press 1988) Vivian Paley noticed how much Frederick, who had a new baby in the family, wanted so much to be the baby in pretend play with his friends. His needs placed some stress on the other children, yet boys as young as four years old often tried to help Frederick to feel better and adapt their play to what he wanted. Vivian Paley described the following sequence:

'When Frederick hears "baby", he rushes into the block area. "I'm the baby tiger." "You can be the daddy tiger," Barney tells him. "No, you said baby."

Christopher tries to help: "Let him be the twin for the other baby, Barney. I'll be the dad." "No twins!" Frederick cries. "I'm the only baby." Barney shrugs his shoulders. "Then who do I be?" "You be the mommy for me," Frederick says. "No! I'm the baby tiger because I said it first. You be the mommy." "I hate you guys! I said I was the baby and you won't let me. I hate you! I'm hating you every day from now on." (page 53)

Feelings and moral judgements

Strong feelings like anger and frustration can emerge in strong words and actions. Four-year-olds can begin to learn and use skills of conflict resolution but only if adults support that learning (see page 16). This area of learning is definitely one in which early years practitioners, and any helpful adults, need to reflect on their own reactions and skills and avoid any simple approach based on 'the children ought to…'. Supportive practitioners can help four-year-olds by respecting the feelings expressed and helping children to understand that forms of expression hurt other people, physically or in terms of their feelings.

In an affectionate and supportive environment, four-year-olds start to be able to link events with feelings, such as, 'I'm cross with him because he knocked my tower down!' They do have some understanding of the feelings of others. Children show this grasp sometimes by comments that are not directly about feelings, but that reveal an underpinning understanding of the role of emotions, that somebody else might be upset by a turn of events.

For example

In New River Green Centre a conversation unfolded between a practitioner and more than one child. They wanted to express concern to the practitioner that a young boy had Megan's special handbag that she had brought in today (see the example on page 27 The practitioner took what the children said with seriousness and reassured them with, 'He's her brother. That's all right, she's allowed him to have her bag.' Megan, who was close by, confirmed that the younger child was her brother and that she had given him permission.

There was a short pause and then another child noticed that the same younger brother was wearing only his socks, saying, 'he hasn't got his shoes on'. The practitioner thanked the child who spoke and said to the younger boy, 'you need your shoes'. The boy (two years old) co-operatively got off his bike, went up to the outdoor shelf full of wellington boots and found his pair. He put them on and returned to his bike.

In order to be a genuine support to children's learning, practitioners need to tune into four-year-old thinking. They are beginning to make some sense of people and experiences beyond their daily life. But they have to be allowed to make the personal connection; you cannot hurry the process. Careful use of small group circle time can work, as can using supports like puppets or Persona Dolls. However, you have to keep your plans realistic for any discussion time with children.

For example

It is possible to see how threes and fours make very personal connections in one particular sequence shown in the video/DVD *Persona Dolls in Action*. The practitioner is introducing Polly, a doll who needs a wheelchair. The young children are interested and want to make connections with their own lives and homes. They show an ability to understand some of what it could be like to be physically disabled, but they still want to share their own personal perspective. The practitioner is sensitive and enables these young children to make the personal connections, as well as introducing Polly's own personal narrative.

Emotional and moral development go hand in hand for young children. The whole business of understanding right and wrong – and trying to take the right path at least some of the time – is interwoven with fours' understanding about feelings as well as actions.

Four-year-olds still tend to have a working theory that everyone will follow the same rules or codes of behaviour. They learn steadily from experience that not all adults set the same rules nor the same consequences for rule-breaking. Four-year-olds also notice when the same adult or adults are not consistent in applying the rules. Children will then, not surprisingly, push out the boundaries.

Children of this age still tend to judge how 'bad' actions are by the seriousness of the consequences. However, their outlook is not only limited by their conceptual grasp of the idea. Many adults make considerably more fuss about larger messes and more extensive damage, so children's moral judgement accurately reflects some of their daily observations.

In a supportive family or early years environment, four-year-olds are more able to allow for and forgive on the basis of the other person's intentions. Four-year-olds may be able to accept that, 'It was an accident' or 'He didn't mean to knock the drink over your painting'. The link to intentions has to be fairly obvious and not be part of a repeating pattern. Otherwise, four-year-olds will sometimes make the judgement that 'he keeps doing that; he must be more careful' or that an adult should stop a younger child who 'is messing up our game!'

Four-year-olds, and three-year-olds too, have often grasped the concept of 'fair' and will launch the criticism of 'that's not fair'. Fairness matters to young children and they cease to respect adults who make a big fuss about behaviour that is 'fair' or 'nice' and then behave in ways themselves that are manifestly unfair.

Four-year-olds may be able to contribute in a supported group discussion, for instance in circle time, to develop or review sensible rules for their group. The more articulate three-year-olds may also actively contribute, but the children will be varied in their ability. They may also be far more punitive about consequences than the adults!

Four-year-olds are learning about behaviour, right and wrong and awareness of the feelings of others. Helpful adults need to tune into four-year-old thinking, respect what children can manage and avoid expectations of consistently 'good' behaviour that would most likely not be met by adults, let alone young children.

- Four-year-olds have often grasped some underlying reasoning for acceptable and unacceptable patterns of behaviour. But these reasons will be voiced in straightforward and practical terms. Children understand logic like, 'we put the toys back where they belong, because then we can all find them again', 'we use the sand timer on the bikes because it's fair, then everyone can have a go' and 'you don't say that word because it is unkind and words can hurt you just as much as being hit'.
- Four-year-olds do not grasp abstract reasons that are unconnected with events and relationships they understand. Nor do four- or five-year-olds need to be able to voice complex reasons in order to show that they have developed a level of prosocial behaviour.
- There is not always a neat match between what four-year-olds may be able to say is the right thing to do and actually doing it. There are many reasons why it can be hard to do the right thing, if you are four years old. It is sobering to recall that there is usually an imperfect match between what grown-ups say they would do, if faced by an imaginary scenario, and what they actually do in real life.

Children and the local community

Four-year-olds have begun to have a sense of themselves that extends into their local neighbourhood and the people and places that they know. Their identity is grounded in their own network of family and friends and this experience may give the beginnings of some grasp of social and cultural group and faith, if this is of relevance to this child's family.

Young children are often interested in slightly different events and experiences that can connect with what makes sense to them: going to nursery or school, family celebrations and shared events like weddings or the arrival of a new baby. In a neighbourhood that is ethnically diverse, four-year-olds will be gaining an idea that not all families look and live like their own. Four-year-olds can also grasp some understanding through play materials and projects that further away from their neighbourhood people and daily life may have many differences. So long as early years settings do not overload the curriculum, then children can begin to build some positive outlooks. But many diverse celebrations and materials about a range of cultures and faiths will only confuse four-year-olds.

The message of the books in this series is consistently to focus on young children now. However, there are times when it is useful to remind yourself of the early learning goal that applies for most children at the end of the Early Years Foundation Stage. For PSED the two relevant ELGs are:

- Understand that people have different needs, views, cultures and beliefs, which need to be treated with respect.
- Understand that they can expect others to treat their needs, views, cultures and beliefs with respect.

The issue of cultural identity also arises within Knowledge and Understanding of World and the relevant ELG here is:

- Begin to know about their own cultures and beliefs and those of other people.

Look closely at those goals – still for an age group older than the focus of this book. Realistic expectations are about a general understanding of difference, a positive sense of identity for all children and two-way respect. Understanding by children of their own culture is at a 'begin to' stage – let alone their grasp of less familiar cultural backgrounds.

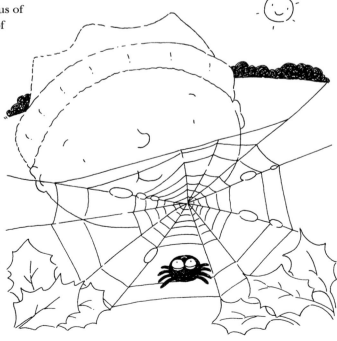

So practitioners need to focus on what makes sense to young children – start with four-year-olds' understanding of their own immediate community and work outwards. As you open the doors to new experiences, make sure that there are strong connections of meaning for children. For instance:

- Experience of a few celebrations can extend children's horizons beyond their own back yard. But you and your colleagues need to make choices; a long list of celebrations will leave children confused and the whole group 'celebrated out'.
- Set a good example to the children by showing respect and an effort to understand traditions that are unfamiliar to you. Be careful not to explain an

unfamiliar celebration by assuming it is much the same as a tradition more familiar to you.

- Involve parents and the local community in any celebration and be ready to learn from them when that is possible and the other adults are happy to talk.
- Explain to parents how you treat celebrations in your setting. If parents still feel strongly that they do not want their child to take part in a given celebration, it may be more respectful to let the child opt out. Any celebration should be brief; children get fed up with projects that last forever, so there should be no consequence that a child missed a great deal of nursery time or learning activities.
- Celebrations should be relaxed and children have choices. Four-year-olds do not develop positive attitudes if they associate a celebration with 'we all had to make the same card!' Equally important, celebrations should be respected in their own right; they do not just exist to support early years topic planning.

Support children in a sense of wonder

Four-year-olds are ready to be thrilled and enchanted, especially in the outdoors. They are intrigued by natural materials, such as mud and water, by magical sights like a rainbow, or a clear view of the stars and the endearing antics of baby birds or animals. Unfortunately, their feelings can be blunted by dismissive adults who say things like, 'what's so interesting about..?' or 'put it down, it's mucky!'

You can support children's sense of wonder and their wish to enjoy, look and listen.

- Join children in what they want to show you. Four-year-olds are far more likely to listen and learn from adults who have a good track record of showing genuine interest in what has caught the child's attention.
- If four-year-olds are keen to watch how worms get into the crumbly earth or how the condensation forms on the window, then they are ready to learn from this experience. When adults tell them to come and do something else, the message is that the child's interest is of no account to the adult.
- Avoid the feeling that as an adult you have to make informative comments or ask questions right now. If children ask you questions then answer. You can contribute simple comments that show you have noticed the details and are pleased the child called this sight to your attention.
- Sometimes children want to explore and find more information right this moment, but often not. You will help by remembering what you shared and helping a child to make connections at a later date, perhaps suggesting you could all create a wormery or letting a child know that you have not forgotten by reminiscing, 'I was remembering when we...'

For example

Four-year-olds who are given time to relax and look are intrigued by many sights, especially outdoors. Their comments as well as their steady looking and listening should remind adults that young children are ready to wonder. Perhaps sometimes we just need to slow down and listen.

- The Rising Sun Woodland project shows (through the video materials and supporting booklet) how these three- and four-year-olds, confident in the outdoor space, wanted to spend time watching an insect moving on a plant, the ripples on the pond or intriguing fungi. The children's comments are refreshing. The sun streaming through the leaves of an elder tree brought the cry of, 'look, look, the tree's on fire!' An impressively large mushroom was described by one child as 'an ear mushroom', which apparently was similar to the old country name for this fungus.

- In training workshops I sometimes ask for anecdotes from early years practitioners to highlight what enchants three- and four-year-olds. There are always plenty of examples, often but not always from outdoor experiences. Children are ready to look, listen and to show a sense of wonder. They want to take time to experience scuttling minibeasts, beautiful or smelly plants and shrubs. They notice the morning dew on plants and grass, the sparkling of moisture on a spider's web, or that the trees are crying (an insightful remark made by a child to a childminder about weeping willows).

Communication, Language and Literacy

By now, four-year-olds have a substantial vocabulary such that they are likely to recognise words they do not yet know and ask, 'what's that word mean?' or 'what did you say?' Some children notice fine differences and may want to know, 'why do you call that a mug? It's a cup.' Many four-year-olds develop personal interests, pursued through books, play activities and some television programmes. You would not expect four-year-olds to have the same vocabulary since some of them will have extended into words that reflect their interest in trucks, cars, dinosaurs, sharks and other scary fish or different kinds of animals.

The skills of spoken communication

Four-year-olds can show a wide use of their language and behave in ways that show they regard language as a tool at their disposal. They use words to express thoughts, plans and possibilities in their play or involvement in meaningful routines. Four-year-olds still need to speak interesting thoughts out loud and find it hard to keep quiet and wait when something has intrigued them.

Four-year-olds use their powers of language to direct their play and organise each other in physical or imaginative activities. Their language serves a real social purpose in guiding their games and enjoyable interaction. Four-year-olds can be sufficiently confident that they play with words and apply their skills within tuneful exchanges (see the examples on page 55).

But they vary in their level of confidence and some will be more reticent. In a familiar context, many four-year-olds will be happy to speak up and sometimes contribute a song or rhyme. But there is nothing to gain and much to lose by putting pressure on children. It is probably not even appropriate to explain a child's refusal in terms of shyness. Some children simply do not want to do anything that feels like performance but are comfortable and communicative in one-to-one or small-scale social groups.

Children's use of language, their comments and questions can be a valuable window onto their ways of thinking. Four-year-olds also show you their expectations, interests and ways of thinking through their behaviour, including play. But their spoken words, especially in a genuine two-way conversation, with you as an adult or overheard between children themselves, can tell you volumes about what is probably going on in four-year-old heads.

For example

Three- and four-year-olds imitate what they find of interest, including adult activity. Some of their pretend play reflects domestic routines but, in early years settings, children are observant of procedures such as the inspection process. Four-year-olds feel that this is their nursery or playgroup and want to know what is happening.

- Jacqui Cousins (in *Listening to Four-Year-Olds*) described how children were interested in what she was doing during her time as what they called an 'Ofsted lady'. In one setting the children

Food for thought

In a 1980s research project, Barbara Tizard and Martin Hughes observed the conversations of four-year-olds in nursery class with their teachers and at home with their mothers. They made the useful distinction that children's thinking develops along two equally important tracks:

- Children need to learn details and they are hungry for information. Children whose enquiries meet with a positive adult response go on to ask other questions when they are ready.
- But four-year-olds are also working hard on a framework to enable them to make sense of the information. Their questions sometimes show an awareness that something does not fit, a sense of, 'but that can't be right because....'

Many of the examples of four-year-olds' questions show evidence of trying out possible theories of how the world works.

The ideas and examples of this research are just as relevant now. Their examples showed how four-year-olds were able to stretch the boundaries to their knowledge by searching questions. Supportive adults can help that stretch when they listen. Barbara Tizard and Martin Hughes talked about the concept of an intellectual search by young children. This idea is very similar to the focus on sustained, shared thinking that is described in the EPPE research papers.

had made small notebooks of their own and sat nearby and observed Jacqui Cousins herself.
- A similar situation happened in the Soho Family Centre in London. Several of the four-year-olds in the pre-school group pulled up their chairs, lined themselves up with the Ofsted inspector's chair and began to make their own observations of the room, writing marks in their notebooks.

Four-year-olds are well able to use their skills of communication to express opinions and preferences. Consultation projects offer many examples of the ways that children can be enabled and encouraged, if necessary, to express views out loud. An often overlooked consequence can be adult surprise, or even unease, at what children say.

- Linda Kinney and Jerry McCabe report some very creative projects that were undertaken in Stirling, Scotland. Visual support with photos, little figures and happy/sad stickers or paper plate faces all ease the process of communication. The visual link makes a connection of meaning for young children and often helps a less confident child to speak their mind. Visual support is also very useful when children are four-year-old fluent in a home language that practitioners do not speak – or not much.
- The Stirling project reports how practitioners found out that some children were experiencing play problems in some areas and would welcome some help. However, the nursery team heard more than they expected when they provided little figures for children to show on the nursery layout where they thought an adult would be helpful. The children named the figures as actual adults and explained why their familiar practitioners were good, or not so good in different roles.
- Another project in Scotland used ICT to supplement the consultation process. Dalry Nursery School in North Ayrshire used a range of simple techniques, including digital cameras and smart boards to support discussion with young children. Again, the children were forthcoming about what worked and what did not work so well in their own setting. The brief report gives the example of one child who said he did not enjoy playing with the small world area because the door on the castle was broken. The practitioner asked him what could be done about this problem and the child replied, 'If you get me a screwdriver, I could fix it' and the report says, 'and he did it!' You can see their report on www.ltscotland.org.uk/earlyyears/sharingpractice/lifeskills/citizenship/dalry/aims.asp

---

Four-year-olds have a good grasp of grammar but are still likely to make some logical mistakes, for example generalising a regular grammatical rule to constructions that do not obey the usual rule. They have usually grasped the power of the negative, along with the appropriate tone of voice, for instance, 'It wasn't me!' or 'I didn't tear the book!' They are able to use words, with the appropriate tone and emphasis, to question and challenge, to tell and explain.

If you listen and note, you will become aware that four-year-olds use their words with a range of different purposes.

...one shoe off and one shoe on, diddle diddle dumpling, my son John.

- Children are now usually able to use their words to tell and describe what is happening in front of them, but also to recount something that has happened from the recent past, with an understanding that this event has happened and gone.
- Four-year-olds are able to ask and request that you or another child do something they wish and often have some of the basic courtesies in words and body language to avoid a sense of demanding.
- They are able to pose questions, sometimes tough ones, and use a questioning tone with comments that flag up to an attentive adult that this is a kind of question. (See also page 26 about four-year-old questions.)

- They use their language to imagine, to create a story or pretend play scenario or to retell a familiar and liked story.
- Four-year-olds are often adept at using language to explain, justify or argue and adults need to admire the use of language even if the four-year-old negotiation skills are still a little raw around the edges.
- They are able sometimes to speculate, wonder about how or why and weigh up some simple possibilities.

Questions, answers and proper conversations

Four-year-olds are capable of the social skills needed for a conversation, so long as their experience has supported their learning. Conversational skills include not only talking, but also pausing to listen, linking what you say to what the other person has just said and being patient to wait your turn. Children learn from adult models, from having people show an interest in what they want to say and being given time to express themselves. Four-year-olds are unlikely to show their conversational skills if they attend an early years setting with a very structured day or session and with adults who feel immense pressure to 'get through the curriculum'.

Collecting children's questions is worthwhile. If they do not ask you many questions, especially if this is the main pattern in the group, then you may need to adjust your communication style. Perhaps you have established the expectation in the children that you ask the questions and they give the answers. Perhaps they think you are too busy; that it is not worth the effort.

For example

In their observations of conversations at home and in nursery Barbara Tizard and Martin Hughes noticed how many topics the four-year-old girls raised in chatting with their mother at home. These young children wanted to know more about many issues, including:

- Why some buildings have sloping roofs and does the rain go through a flat roof
- How to share out a limited number of cakes
- Why little children cry and scream
- How Father Christmas does his job
- Why it is that clocks tell the time but not the day.
- How and why the window cleaner gets paid

Jacqui Cousins continued this line of research with Martin Hughes and other colleagues. The practical issues raised about adult language and role are as relevant as ever. Jacqui Cousins listed a range of penetrating questions that she heard four year olds pose about issues that intrigued or perplexed them at that moment. Just a few of these questions were:

- Where does the water go when it goes down the drain?
- How does a maypole work? Is that thing at the top called a rat-shit? Why?
- Where do worms go when the snow is on the ground? Can they breathe?
- Do daddies ever come back when you never, never knowed them ever?

In her observations, Jacqui Cousins was concerned that powerful four-year-old thinking was not always noticed by practitioners who were over-focused on their own plans for activities.

The examples given within this section show the wide range of issues that can interest four-year-olds. Some examples are taken from conversations that happened within children's own family. (See the examples on pages 44 - 46.) But in a relaxed early years setting, children can be generous in sharing their thoughts and questions. Their comments are a reminder of what four-year-olds are able to explore when they have time and the welcome from adults for proper conversation. Four-year-olds are likely to be more reticent if experience tells them that adults do not listen, or that adults take a child's interest and drive it in another direction. Four-year-olds also need sustained personal conversation engaged with their current interest. Circle or other group time, although useful in some ways, cannot tune into four-year-olds in this personal way.

Barbara Tizard and Martin Hughes pointed out that early years practitioners can seriously underestimate four-year-old thinking power and the richness of their language. The reasons seem to be twofold. Adult time is genuinely more thinly spread in early years settings than in many family homes. But also early years practice can block four-year-old language when the emphasis is far more on adult questions and on compartmentalised learning within an adult plan.

For example

In New River Green Megan (four years old) had brought in a personal item, her handbag. She wanted to show the contents of her handbag to a practitioner who expressed genuine interest and followed Megan's lead. Something family-related in the handbag led to a question from the practitioner about Megan's family, 'I thought you just had one brother?' Megan went on to explain in detail the members of her family and the practitioner listened carefully, reflecting back some of what Megan volunteered.

A short while later Megan was talking with another practitioner about her journey to nursery this morning. Megan said proudly, 'I crossed the road myself. I looked both ways.' The practitioner asked, 'was Mummy beside you' and Megan was firm that, 'I did it myself'. She talked in some detail about how she knew how to cross the road and the practitioner listened, following Megan's lead. Megan also chatted about how she could find her way to nursery and announced, 'I have a map', which she pulled out of her handbag. Later, the practitioner checked discreetly with Megan's mother, who had brought her to nursery. It was clear that Megan was keen to check the road herself and make decisions about crossing, but she was not left alone to do so.

The **REPEY** project illustrated, through the observations in the research, what was meant by sustained shared thinking. The important features help to show how genuinely helpful adults behave in early years settings, and in family homes. The team emphasise that:

- Children learn when they are motivated and involved and it is logical to consider the role of an effective educator in the same way. Effective early years practitioners need to engage with the children and to be genuinely interested in the child's focus. Effective practitioners are motivated and involved, as well as the children.
- The sensitive and responsive practitioner then goes with what interests the child and takes it a little further. The communication and behaviour offers a potential extension; it is not the case that adults insist on a particular direction.

- The adult needs to be as involved as the child, so adult actions and joining in play are important. It is not effective to comment in an uninvolved way from the sidelines.
- Responsive interaction is not achieved by imposed adult plans, worksheets and instruction. In contrast, adults help by becoming part of play and joining in communication by making comments, suggestions, speculations and open-ended questions.

Conversation in a group

Generally four-year-olds like to have a one-to-one conversation or at least a discussion limited to a small number of children with an adult. Otherwise there is too much waiting time and the conversation can take turns that do not directly interest some children. Four-year-olds can manage some small group time, so long as it is sensitively led by a practitioner and this time is not the only opportunity to express views.

Show and tell time or circle time can be a short and enjoyable time for four-year-olds to share in something of general interest and to hear the views of other children, with whom they may not chat normally in the course of a day or session. Circle time can work well in sensitive hands but unfortunately can be a boring or even an unhappy experience for children when the practitioner leading the time is insensitive or follows only the adult agenda (see also page 28 in *What Does it Mean to be Five?*)

Circle time can work for four-year-olds so long as you tune into what is possible and interesting for them. Adults have to be reflective as well as realistic in what they do.
Children appreciate recognition of their skills, for instance with, 'Gareth, that was good waiting. I can see you were very keen to talk' or 'Katie, what a good idea, I can hear that you've been thinking hard'.

Vivian Gussin Paley's books about her practice with threes and fours (in the United States) show she reflected on her role and learned to respect and draw upon children's play. The children's learning was in their play rather than a directive adult role of forever adapting children's ideas to what she, as the nursery teacher, wanted to fit her pre-organised adult plans. Vivian Gussin Paley explains how she used circle time, but had initially viewed this approach as a way for her to raise issues. The content of the small group times was all about what she judged to be important for the children to consider. In reviewing her tape recording of circle time sessions, Vivian Gussin Paley realised that all the themes that genuinely enthused the children had arisen in their play, especially their self-chosen pretend play. They were able, and highly motivated, to talk about feelings, dilemmas and the enduring themes of good and bad arising in fairy tales.

You need ground rules for circle time that are explained to the children and followed by the adults. Practitioners must set a good example.

Rising fours and four-year-olds begin to practise good communication skills such as:

- We listen to each other: using our ears and waiting our turn.
- We look at each other with our eyes, because we learn by looking as well as listening.
- We speak to express our ideas, views and feelings.
- We think with our minds and then express those thoughts in words.
- We concentrate by looking and listening to the adult and our friends.

Helpful adults need to:

- Keep discussion open and follow four-year-old interests and hot topics for them today.
- Vary the content of circle time and ensure that it is not always heavy emotionally.
- Listen to what children say and how they say it. Circle time will not work if practitioners are too keen to talk.
- Be aware that children who trust you, may talk about a personal family issue. Show you have heard, but gently bring an end to the discussion and come back to it with this child in a confidential conversation.
- Circle time should not be used as a time to criticise children in front of their peers. Even if children break one of the communication ground rules, adults need to model courtesy, perhaps with, 'whispering stops us hearing what each person is saying. Let's try that again'.

Bilingual children

Some four-year-olds are already successfully bilingual. Some encounter a language different from their family language when they enter an early years setting. Children cope well and being bilingual is not a problem in itself. It is only monolingual speakers who think bilingualism is different from the norm and problematic. Around the world, not only in the UK, many children have more than one language. However, it is inaccurate to assume that children just 'pick up' a language with no effort. Children whose fluent language is not spoken in nursery, or not by many people, need support as they link up the words, and sometimes a new written script, to familiar objects and events.
In diverse neighbourhoods and settings, monolingual four-year-olds can have understood that not everyone speaks the same language, even that some kinds of writing look different from each other.

Young children have a great capacity for language but practitioners need to challenge some of the less wise suggestions about exploiting this 'window of opportunity'. I have encountered some advice that all children should learn another language in the early years, even when few, if any, people locally speak the language in daily life. It is hard to see any developmental sense in this approach, especially when it means that adults play sound tapes of languages they neither speak nor understand themselves. Children need to make connections, so there is little point in exposing young children to a language that is not embedded in a social context for them.

Children are interested in languages other than their own that they can link with real people. Perhaps Stefan's mum is part Polish and can sing some Polish nursery rhymes or Teja's dad has come in to show a range of Indian scripts.

The importance of conversation

Four-year-olds can be skilled communicators but their competence can be blocked if adults undervalue the learning power of personal communication. Jacqui Cousins has a longstanding research and practical interest in the importance of oral communication. In *Listening to Four-Year-Olds* she summed up her concerns about how some practitioners have lost their way. As the results of hours of careful observation in early years settings, she homed in on the problems that arise when young children's spontaneous conversation is not educationally valued. In too many of the settings, children's own talk was seriously underestimated as a tool for thinking. Many of the practitioners had accepted a role that they needed to ask lots of questions – the same problem identified by Barbara Tizard and Martin Hughes. Those interjections sometimes formed a direct interruption of children's own exploration through words and actions.

Ann Locke and Jane Ginsborg have explored the perspective of early years practitioners through an intervention study to address delayed development of children's skills of verbal language. Their research findings confirmed many of Jacqui Cousins' concerns and her explanation of how practice can go awry. Ann Locke and Jane Ginsborg described their observations that early years practitioners, under a high sense of pressure, risk taking on a kind of educational tunnel vision that 'just talking' with children was wasting precious time. Completing planned activities, especially on literary, was a higher priority than allowing time for child-initiated conversation. Yet children learn through talking, they need to express their thoughts – what Locke and Ginsborg called the inside-out learning - and not only listen to adults – the outside-in learning.

Over-planning in the early years curriculum can lead to the strange situation in which practitioners say that they have not done any 'communication activities' today, when they mean there was nothing on the plan that related directly to language and communication.

- Communication and opportunities for listening and talking should be on-going. Children need to be able to relax, have places where it is comfortable to chat and times and routines that promote relaxed conversational exchange.
- Four-year-olds do not need structured programmes, unless their language is delayed or developmentally awry. Language is social and needs to be grounded in a meaningful context for talk.
- The give and take of normal conversation can unfold through shared activities. You need ordinary events in which children and adults are engaged and enthused, dealing with practical problems to solve, memories to recall and share and the expression of ideas and opinions.

Realistic expectations for early literacy skills

The descriptive highlights in the EYFS about four-year-olds and early literacy focus on:

- Continued support for crucial skills of oral communication and alert listening. The emphasis continues to be on personal interaction, conversation and alertness to rhythm and sound patterns.
- Enthusiasm for stories with detailed recall of familiar tales and child-initiated use of books. Active involvement in story telling by different means that can take a creative leap for fours. A detailed understanding of how books work – both fiction and information books – and the flow of written text.
- A sharp awareness of sounds and sound patterns in the language(s) familiar to children. Fours are adept at detailed recall of familiar songs and rhymes. But they create their own version and play around with sounds, showing a grasp of rhythm and sound patterns.
- Clearer understanding about deliberate mark making and an ability to distinguish between drawing – their own and illustrations in books – and writing. Early literacy skills move towards emergent writing over this year.
- Significant awareness of the meaning of print in their familiar environment: whole words, familiar logos and an increasing range of letters that have personal significance.

Older fours – and some younger fours – can be very competent and well on the road to literacy skills that parents will recognise as 'proper' reading and writing. However, England stands pretty much alone in the imposition of an early years curriculum framework that sets up the expectation that fives will be able to read and write. Ann Locke and Jane Ginsborg are just two, of a considerable number of early years specialists, who point out the serious developmental consequences when young children are not enabled to spend their early years mainly focusing on spoken language skills. In many other European countries, children do not start formal school until six years of age. In England, and some other parts of the UK, many fours attend provision on school grounds. When that daily experience is very structured, young children effectively risk losing two years of vital time for oral communication skills.

Impressive four-year-olds skills

Over the months that they are four, children can add to a wide range of early literacy skills:

- They can enjoy fiction through story books and use their own language to retell a story or event. They often recount familiar stories following a book accurately page by page.
- Children may make meaningful marks that they regard as 'my writing'. They are likely to be able to get close to some letters, especially those that have meaning for them, for example in their own name.
- There are a group of physical skills that underpin writing and reading: the combination of looking, scanning, holding and pencil control. Four-year-olds are likely to be experimenting with different grips on a pencil or crayon and with a comfortable, workable writing position. They need and benefit from relaxed practice, with large physical movements as well as fine co-ordinations.
- Four-year-olds can have some understanding of the symbolic nature of letters of the alphabet, that they stand for sounds that children already know from spoken language.
- Four-year-olds can also have worked out that numbers are a different symbol system. However, a great deal depends on children's experiences so far. A grasp of the symbolic nature of writing does not appear just because they pass their fourth birthday.
- Four-year-olds are likely to be in the process of understanding that letters are put together to form words and that those words then build into sentences. People write messages that have meaning and written material all around us gives information.
- Children are in the process of working out what reading is and how you learn to read (see page 31). It is not obvious to them initially that, although written words may support the pictures in a book, it is the actual words that are read for the story.
- Talking and thinking are crucial underpinning skills for literacy. Children who have plenty to talk about, who weigh up and plan and explore in words will have more material to write about. They still have to learn the technical skills, but writing needs content as well. Literacy is supported when four-year-olds are encouraged to talk and plan what will be written, at this age by dictating to adults.

Early years practitioners, as well as parents, need to see and understand the 'story' of how young children unravel the mysteries of written language. Detailed observations of what individual children do over the months, and years, provide the window onto how children are best helped to tackle this important, but very challenging task. English is an especially difficult language and children need more – not less – time before formal literacy teaching than if they were learning a more standard language.

I strongly recommend the narrative of Alice's learning, provided by Robin Campbell (her grandfather as well as an early years specialist). In the year up to her fifth birthday Alice developed her skills to write some words, to recognise others on the computer screen and to recognise some single letters. Alice could read (rather than tell from memory) some familiar books or parts of a story. She liked to create stories, some of which she would write or type and then ask for help as she dictated the rest.

Alice's early years in her family gave her easy access to books, being read to and generous amounts of stationery for her mark making. She has the building blocks of literacy in place. But it is important to realise that she is doing well for a nearly five-year-old. Her capabilities show the positive effect of adult support and a relaxed experience of early literacy in the home. Some of the youngest children will be only just five years old at the end of the EYFS. Alice, although doing well, has not reached the more challenging interpretation that is sometimes taken of the reading and writing early learning goals. Also – linking with the important points made by Ann Locke and Jane Ginsborg – Alice had experienced a learning environment rich in speaking and listening. She had not honed her literacy skills instead of oral communication; they had developed alongside each other.

Keen mark makers

Anne Hughes and Sue Ellis highlight how children need to learn how writing is used, as well as how they can write: 'Problems may arise if the quest for perfect letter formation becomes a barrier to children understanding the other aspects of writing: the pleasure that writing can give to writer and reader; the power it has to influence actions; the composition skills and knowledge required for writing for different purposes etc. In short how writing is used in the adult world.' (page 5, *Writing it Right*)

Four-year-olds can steadily learn that there is a standard way of writing and they need adults to make explicit what letters look like, how to form the letters, the relationship between the letter symbols and sounds, and how letters are grouped together to form words. In order to help four-year-olds, adults themselves need to be able to consider literacy in all its separate parts.

Parents often feel that learning to read and write is a technical skill best taught by 'experts'. Consequently, they easily underestimate how much children learn at home through ordinary activities. Early years practitioners can support the confidence of parents by explaining and showing how much children need to connect the technical skills with everyday use of literacy.

For example

Good early years practice has always used practical ways for young children to apply their emerging literacy skills - for reasons that make sense to the children themselves.

* Louise Davies of Town and Country Kiddies described to me the normal routine in her nurseries. Each day a child uses the internal phone to call the nursery cook and find out the details of the menu for the day.

Food for thought

It is important to consider what four-year-olds are learning about literacy, and not only the different skills that will build towards confident reading and writing. Four-year-olds are developing their attitudes; this development is not only about technical skills.

You want children to feel that reading and writing are useful skills for the future as well as now. When there is great pressure from adults on children, especially from a young age, there is a serious risk that children feel they are learning to read and write solely because adults want them to achieve this skill. In a worst case scenario, children then learn to read (or write) in order to stop reading. They develop the idea that adults nag them to read and once you have done it, they will leave you alone.

A different set of attitudes are likely to develop when four-year-olds can observe how familiar adults use their reading and writing skills in daily activities. They can learn there is a point to personal literacy skills; they will be useful. Appropriate experiences over early childhood can build secure foundations for early literacy skills and understanding.

Children themselves then draw and 'write' the menu on their board. Discussion then often follows between the children about what they will be eating later and their views about the upcoming meal. Children are at ease with expressing opinions and making decisions. Another part of the usual routine is that they make final decisions on each day about what will be laid out in some of the spaces of their nursery.

Fours, and young children, develop their own early literacy skills, with no need for any pressure, when application and practice of emergent reading and writing is a natural part of daily experience – and not a separate adult-led activity.

In The Grove Nursery School the team had thought carefully about making materials portable for children. Children had generous resources of writing and general stationery materials, but the nursery team accepted that writing materials should not have to stay in the graphics area. They wanted children to feel confident that writing did not just happen in the literacy area or in 'literacy activities'.

- They encouraged children to take writing resources to where they wanted to write.
- They took the trouble to acknowledge children's skills when they were used. Children were given on-the-spot feedback with friendly comments like, 'that's good reading' or 'excellent use of tools there' and so on.
- I have encountered, and read about, other settings, whose teams have thought creatively. The firm plastic-handled tool boxes can be ideal for creating an outdoor discovery box or a maths and measuring box, as well as the travelling writing materials.
- The great advantage of the travelling materials is that children are more likely to consider that such skills are transferable. Four-year-olds begin to believe that meaningful mark making is a useful skill for a wide range of activities. Measuring and counting are handy skills for all kinds of activities and games.
- In contrast, if materials are kept firmly in one place, children may decide that writing only happens at the writing table and when adults ask you to do a writing activity.

Understanding the task for four-year-olds

Adults can be egocentric about early literacy, failing to grasp the perspective of four-year-olds, for whom the skills and the underlying concepts are still not clear. Penny Munn's research has highlighted the importance of children's beliefs about reading. She has described well the shift from children's belief that reading is a kind of 'book-aided story repetition' to understanding that you have to decode the actual print. It is a positive development when children learn stories by heart, and shared story telling is an enjoyable activity, but children need to grasp that memorising a story is not the same as reading.

Penny Munn interviewed children several times (aged three and then four years of age) about their understanding of reading over the year before they went to primary school (in Scotland). The children replied each time to four questions: 'can you read?', 'who do you know who can read?', 'when will you be able to read?' and ' what will you have to do to be able to read?' The changes in children's beliefs over that year are an intriguing window onto the thinking of fours. In brief, Penny Munn found that:

- Most of the children started the year already familiar with story books. But they believed, at the outset, that reading was about turning the pages and telling a story. By the end of the year many more children, but not all, showed an understanding that reading actually meant decoding print: that the written text was the explicit source of the story.
- Not surprisingly, quite a few of the young fours thought they could read already, because they believed that reading was the same as recounting a familiar story with the book in your hand. About a year later, many of these now older children realised that 'reading' was more than knowing a book by heart.
- The four-year-olds who were familiar with books, from home and not only nursery, were less daunted by realising that actually they could not yet read. Children with a family background low in literacy appeared less confident and more likely to find ways to avoid the risk of 'failure'.

Problem Solving, Reasoning and Numeracy

This new title in the EYFS for this area of development is a useful recognition that four-year-olds' grasp of early mathematical ideas is best grounded in practical problem solving, often within their play. Young children need to be allowed to make steady progress, much like their development within literacy. Adults need to recognise and show that they appreciate the steps along the way and resist the temptation to push children along too fast – although there is considerably less harassment about early numeracy than over early literacy. Nevertheless, undue pressure will certainly disrupt the process of learning and risks leaving even young children convinced that, 'I'm no good at maths'.

Impressive four-year-old skills

The descriptive highlights in the EYFS about four-year-olds focus on:

- Using their spontaneous language for number and counting – being interested in this skill and often using their eyes to know 'how many' items they have.
- Having a broad vocabulary to talk about size, shape, time or other concepts – but still linked with objects and experiences in their familiar environment.
- Looking carefully and being able to see similarities of amount, size, shape and then choosing appropriately for their building or measuring task.
- Using close observation and their own words to compare and contrast – an increasingly sophisticated understanding of relative size, weight, speed and other concepts that have meaning in their play and regular domestic routines.
- Using basic mathematical concepts to explore and solve problems in play – organising materials and people, counting or measuring for a reason.
- Recognition of some numbers lower than ten and working out soon that these symbols are different from letters. (There is no expectation that children will learn to write numbers before the end of the EYFS.)
- Using many examples of basic positional or directional language and understanding simple instructions or games led by these words.

Practical maths makes sense to four-year-olds

Four-year-olds can have strong foundations to mathematical ideas but they need them to be connected to what they understand so far. A regular problem for children arises when early years practitioners, and other adults like parents, hurry to the more abstract ideas of number, shape and numerical operations. These ideas only feel obvious to adults because our minds are familiar with them. But the ideas and how you handle them are brand new to four-year-olds.

Margaret Donaldson offered an insight into how seriously confused children can get. The more formal style of school-based learning requires from children what she called 'disembedded thinking'. By this Margaret Donaldson meant that schools require a particular way of thinking from children, in which ideas are separate from the context familiar to young children. Throughout childhood, older children steadily learn to step back from the familiar and concrete application of ideas. Yet when they are younger than five or six years, a high level of abstraction simply makes no sense to them. Margaret Donaldson first wrote about disembedded thinking in the 1970s. Her insights are even more crucial as changes in the 1990s have brought more formal and structured approaches into the early years.

- An unwise pressure of 'earlier must be better' has brought high risks of confusion for children who are pushed to take on board mathematical concepts without context.
- Unreflective adults can assume that four- and five-year-olds are being dense and awkward, even that completion of a planned mathematical activity must assure that children have learned the ideas.
- Yet uncritical application of the ideas of Jean Piaget has led to the opposite mistake: that of believing that four- and five-year-olds are unable to grasp many mathematical ideas because of their intellectually 'egocentric' outlook. A more accurate view of the thinking power of four-year-olds is somewhere in between these two extremes.

Martin Hughes' studies of early mathematical skills demonstrate the impressive thinking power of four-year-olds, as well as the point at which confusion blurs children's understanding. In one study, Martin Hughes showed that well over half of the three- and four-year-olds could manage hypothetical ('what if...') counting, so long as the imaginary situation that was described in words made sense and related to children's own experience. So this age group could often give the correct answer to a question such as, 'if there were two girls in a shop and another one went in, how many girls would be in the shop now?' The children could transform the words into a familiar visual image in their imagination and often manage the correct answer, although they had nothing in front of them to count. Fours really struggle with disembedded questions like, 'what is two and one more?'

For example

Young children show you what they understand in this area of development, if you just watch and listen to what they do in their child-initiated play and conversation. Fours also choose to get involved in interesting adult-initiated experiences and resources that are added to their learning environment in a flexible way.

One afternoon in Buckingham's Nursery, I observed how much children enjoyed working with a large sheet of paper, held secure by tyres out in the garden, and accompanied by a generous store of wax crayons.

- Children were very interested to make marks, draw and to 'brass rub' the pattern that came through from the texture of the hard surface. Several children used colour words spontaneously or were able to find me a particular colour when I asked for 'help' in my search for a specific colour crayon. (Colour is not a mathematical concept; this part of the observation is simply a reminder that more is always going on than learning in a single area of development.)
- Four-year-old Gaby had drawn a butterfly – she told me that was what it was – and asked me to draw one. I asked her to tell me how to draw a butterfly like the one she had just showed me. Gaby was able to use her words to explain what I had to do and in what order. She was also confident to correct my potential 'mistakes', when I made a shape above the paper to ask if this looked right. She also used shape words, in particular a circle, to instruct me on how

Being a helpful adult

Four-year-olds need to see the point of numbers and other mathematical operations. They need a sense that numbers are all around them: the practical concept of environmental maths, like Cathy Nutbrown's idea of environmental print.

- Children build their understanding when adults use mathematical talk in a natural way, directly connected to activities, tasks or problem-solving that can be seen directly in front of you and the children.
- In a similar way to voicing literacy out loud you need to make your maths explicit. Without talking all the time, of course, you can show what you do with your own mathematical abilities. It helps children if you speak your thoughts out loud and explain why you need to count or measure this time.
- You express the ideas of basic maths out loud in your spoken words and through commenting briefly on your actions: counting, time and time passing, whether something fits, comments on same and different.
- Sensible use of comments and open-ended questions can enable you to check that children's understanding is in step with your own: the ideas of 'Are we looking at this in the same way?' and 'Are we all talking about the same thing?'

Being a helpful adult

As adults we have lived with a wide range of abstract ideas for many years. Mathematical ideas of number, shape, size, speed and qualities like colour or texture seem obvious to us. Unless we give time to reflect and observe children, we can fail to tune into the current thinking of a four-year-old.

- You need to push aside for a short while what we know and understand as adults. You need to use your adult thinking power to imagine from time to time what it must be like not to know or understand what are now very familiar ideas to you.
- Remember that what seems so obvious to you as an adult is far from obvious to a four-year-old. Children's learning is not helped if we press on regardless with words or body language that communicate, 'But it's so obvious!' But it is not obvious, otherwise children would not have that puzzled or unhappy expression on their face.
- You need to start from the point that this child has reached with their understanding and not from some stage that they 'ought' to be.

to build up the butterfly from several circle shapes. With the help of Gaby's shared strategy, I produced a better butterfly than I would have done on my own!

Incidentally these same resources were later fully enjoyed by two-year-olds later in the same afternoon – a useful reminder that appropriate open-ended resources work well across the age range.

A considerable amount of early learning within this aspect of development happens easily through play when children have time to become absorbed and adult comments follow the child's lead of actions or words. Familiar resources like sand and water are a perfect resource, since children explore the natural materials and can be heard spontaneously using their own language for position, fit and size. Sand and water, with simple containers and other equipment, provide young children with direct, hands-on exploration of all the early mathematical concepts that arise from filling, emptying, building and creating shapes in the sand.

- In Buckingham's Nursery I observed a great deal of spontaneous discussion between three children who wanted to make a Halloween cake with the sand - using basic mathematical language around 'that's enough' or 'we need some more'. A slightly different discussion about enough, full and empty arose from the children's enthusiasm for watering the garden. The large water butt in their garden is not an endless source of water. So the children experienced that even a container this large will be empty eventually and stay that way until someone refills it from the hose. The watering cans hung on hooks fixed to the fence and this provided a regular experience for children of one-to-one correspondence because they were encouraged to tidy cans back onto the hooks.
- Further outdoor exploration was possible because of the outline shapes marked permanently onto the flat surface of the lower garden. I observed an enthusiastic game when an adult and several children were stepping carefully around the outline shapes marked on the flat surface. The adult did not comment on the shape – name or otherwise – and I think that judgment was right, because the children were absorbed in direct experience of the sides of the shapes. Practitioners make many of-the-moment decisions about whether to comment on what children are doing. The right decision is sometimes not to say anything and be a playful companion to children, who in this instance were very busy doing a triangle and the other shapes.
- I also observed a lively obstacle course game involving tyres, the mini-slide and hoops on the ground. While I was watching the adult was counting hoops with the children as they stepped through them and then again as the children climbed and balanced on each tyre in turn.
- At another point in the day, there was an energetic game with the hoops, when children were persistent, and occasionally successful, in rolling a hoop along the ground. The adult rolled four or five hoops at the same time – a striking effect - and at a 'ready steady go' from her the children ran after them. This fun activity provided direct experience for children of the operation of a plaything that is circular. Again the adult focused on the enjoyment and lively running and I think that was appropriate. Physically active children would probably have been distracted by comments about circle or circular. They were busy with direct experience of what happens when a circular shape can be rolled.
- On another day I was sitting inside with a small group of four-year-olds who chose to show me a set of pictures, all of which had a deliberate mistake – not always very obvious. These young children were interested to look closely at most of the pictures in the set, some more than once. The children showed sharp looking skills and were sometimes able to explain why something was so wrong. One child was very clear about why square wheels would not work on a bicycle – that they would not 'go round' and so the bike could not move.

Practical research, about how young children develop their mathematical ideas, can really help early years practitioners to tune into four-year-old understanding. Summaries like that of Dorothy Caddell's Numeracy in the Early Years (full reference on page 65) support professionals who are unlikely to track the original research reports. Practical researchers like Penny Munn show what works – for instance, that four-year-olds had built up a considerable amount of genuine mathematical knowledge through everyday routines and games that used numbers. Often these activities were more common at home than in early years settings. Yet parents often underestimated how much they supported their children's early mathematical understanding because their adult view was that maths was done by 'experts' in early years and school settings.

Observation of four-year-olds shows that many of them have an extensive knowledge of counting words, how to count and the order of numbers in a sequence. Fours can often read and write some numbers. Penny Munn reported that they understood basic number operations such as adding, subtracting and sharing out. But, the key point was that four-year-olds had come to understand these abstract ideas within a meaningful and practical context. Such findings highlight that it is crucial that early years and school practitioners use their skills of observation, in order to establish what the children know and understand, rather than working on unchecked assumptions.

Early numeracy, just like early literacy, has to be interactive. Young children engage with practical tasks and materials (not worksheets) and with shared routines in which children have an active role to play in collaboration with their peers and with adults. Young children initially confuse saying and reading the numerals with actual counting. There are parallels for four year old understanding with their belief at first that re-telling the story is the same as reading (see page 35).

Understanding more about number

Four-year-olds can have a good grasp of practical number and an understanding of usefulness of counting. Their learning progresses a step at a time and children of a similar age will show diverse skills.

- As Penny Munn has demonstrated, four-year-olds are in the process of working out the nature of numbers, how and why we count. Observant adults who listen to children can gain a sense of what children understand about the process as well as the concepts.
- In this area of learning, as so many others, four-year-olds are having to work out what is important and what is not. For instance, in terms of what makes something five, some children believe for a while that the layout of the dots on a large dice is the crucial feature. They may then argue that it cannot be five if the dots are in a different pattern. Children are exploring what makes 'fiveness'; that it is how many items and not the layout that is initially the most familiar to them.
- Four-year-olds can be relatively confident in counting 'how many?' They need plenty of practice in number order and some four-year-olds have grasped that you count up, and down, in the same pattern each time. So six follows five each time when you are counting higher numbers.
- Many four-year-olds have understood that numbers have meaning in a one-to-one correspondence, although some are still confused. Many four-year-olds with practical experience know now that, if you want five bits of wood, you stop counting at five, rather than go on and on until you run out of the numbers you know.

Food for thought

Children's ability to understand and respond to time is more than being able to 'tell the time'. Jacqui Cousins' observations showed how fours were very aware of the pressures of time, imposed on them by adults who tried to pack too much into the day or session. Her research provides examples, which are profoundly sad to read, of children who explain how they do not bother to play with some favourite resources in their early years setting, because they are never allowed enough time to play properly.

A serious misunderstanding, that creates the 'hurry up, hurry up' scenario, seems to arise when teams do not trust learning through child-initiated play. Practitioners feel obligated to ensure that children experience the set programme, pre-determined by adults. So, absorbed children are harried to move on, or to tidy up their project, because the written plan is that they experience another aspect of the early years curriculum right now.

The EYFS guidance confirms what was always the case with the Foundation Stage: that children can learn in all the developmental areas by focussing on what interests them during this session or day. One experience, undertaken with enthusiasm by children and supported sensitively by adults, will flow into many different skills and new connections.

- Children have the practical skills that help guide application of their knowledge. Counting by finger pointing, or physically moving the bits of wood, help children to keep track of where they are in this counting task.
- Some but not all four-year-olds can recognise some numbers and distinguish them from letters. They may be able and want to write some numbers within a meaningful practical task.

Understanding numbers in money

Money is a complex part of mathematical thinking, yet four-year-olds have some understanding, as well as confusion. Part of understanding money is about the numbers, but money value is more complex.

- Four-year-olds can surprise adults in the extent they understand money and value, when the application is part of a practical discussion (see the example below).
- Understanding money also involves grasping the symbolic function of coins and notes, including the illogical fact (from children's perspective) that the largest coins are not necessarily those with the highest purchasing value.
- Four-year-olds, who accompany adults on high street trips to the bank or post office and who witness the use of cash machines, take another step in trying to grasp money ideas, when cash appears in an almost magical way.

For example

Four-year-olds can be very competent in managing the number work involved in money, so long as they have a realistic situation through which to connect what they know so far. Some of their explorations are through play and you will hear some lively exchanges in a pretend shop or post office. However, Judy Miller describes some financial planning led by an adult with a group of two-, three- and four-year-olds.

- The children were directly involved in choosing play materials from a catalogue for their crèche. The children were told the budget limit and they had the same number of discs as the total pounds limit. The practitioner supported the children as they offered choices and then counted out the number of discs that they would have to pay for this item. The presence of actual pretend coins enabled these young children to see how much 'money' would go from their budget in order to pay for particular items. They were able to discuss, and move pretend coins to and fro, until they reached an agreed shopping list. The children then made the trip into town with a practitioners and purchased the toys that had been agreed.

Judy Miller provides many instances of ways to invite young children into direct involvement in their own early years setting. I have encountered other examples when adults take simple steps, such as using visuals, to enable children to make sense of otherwise rather abstract ideas. I have been told about growing and gardening projects in nurseries and primary schools, where children are brought fully on board about how much money is available for buying seeds or plants. Fours and older children soon become skilled at working out what 'we can get people to give us', so that the limited amount of money is spent wisely. But I think many adults still underestimate the ability of fours to take considered financial decisions, when direct experience enables them to see what something costs. The tendency of even older children to think that adults have an endless supply of money (which they are too mean to share) often arises because nobody has involved children in real decisions about a budget that affects them.

Understanding time

Four-year-olds rarely understand clock time and it is not unusual for six- or seven-year-olds to still be confused about telling the time. But an understanding of time is much more than clock time and adults can support young children as they understand this concept.

- Four-year-olds learn concepts of time through familiarity with routines. Pleasantly predictable routines enable them to understand the sequence of events within a day or session and the meaningful passing of time.
- Four-year-olds understand time related to what can be fitted into a time slot, like one more circuit of the garden on the bike, before 'five minutes' makes much sense. They also understand the use and value of simple time measuring devices such as large sand timers.
- Children's understanding of exact time is not greatly helped by adult sloppiness, as understandable as that may be. How long is the favourite adult concept of 'just a minute'?
- Four-year-olds' language also begins to reflect the vocabulary of time with words and phrases for parts of the day like 'morning' and 'afternoon' and time indicators such as 'soon', 'later on', 'when' and 'how long will you be?'
- A level of predictability about what happens on days of the week enables some four-year-olds to grasp the pattern that Monday comes before Tuesday and that some events like nursery do not happen at the weekend.

Knowledge and Understanding of the World

Being a helpful adult

Questions can be useful in a genuine two-way conversational exchange, but a narrow adult use of questions rarely helps young children to learn. Unfortunately a testing/checking style of question can develop in early years settings and creates an unspoken ground rule that adults ask the questions and children give the answers.

Testing questions are asked by adults to check that children know something. Margaret Donaldson suggests that such questions are part of shifting children into the role of pupil, as envisaged by many teachers. But this style blocks the learning of four-year-olds. Concerns have also been raised about the preponderance of adult talk and questions in Reception and Year 1 classes as teachers feel the pressure to deliver the National Literacy Strategy (see page 35 in *What Does it Mean to be Five?*)

Some children recognise the oddity of adults who ask many questions to which they already know the answer. Jacqui Cousins (*Listening to Four-Year-Olds*) quotes Sonnyboy's challenge to his teacher, 'why do you keep asking us questions when you know all the answers. Like "what colour is it, then?" You can see for yourself it's red, so why do you keep asking?' (page 16)

Four-year-olds can be interested in the world around them and their curiosity by word and action is a powerful support to exploration of all the ideas that later come to be described under school subject headings such as science, geography and history. Learning is supported by children's wish to know and understand. A scientific outlook is strongly supported by four-year-olds' keenness to look, listen and poke. Their imagination is a support, since science operates in some ways as a 'let's pretend' language: 'what if that happened?', 'let's imagine I changed this' or 'let's pretend that I only changed that and nothing else'.

Whose questions matter?

Open communication is crucial, that children feel able to ask questions and to speculate, in contrast to a situation in which they feel obligated to answer adult questions. It can be useful to reflect on your use of questions with children, either as you think about your own individual practice or in team discussions. With thanks to Saplings Nursery, whose team first got me reflecting on questions about questions.

Do you consider sometimes 'is this a genuine question that I am asking?' Ways of checking can be to ask yourself:

- Do I really want to know the answer from the child(ren)?
- Do I already know the answer?
- Does the child have the answer and I do not?

It is well worth considering, 'do I ask a lot of questions?' or 'do I ask a lot of testing questions, to which I know the answer, but I want to know whether the children can give the correct reply?'

Consider :

- Do children give me 'odd' answers? 'Wrong' answers?
- What can I learn from their replies?
- Do the children seem confused but keen to co-operate?
- Do they go silent? Change the subject? Wander off?

Maybe children want to co-operate, but they are confused about what you are asking. Perhaps you and the children are not actually talking about the same thing. Perhaps your question does not connect closely enough, or at all, with their current understanding. That is why the children look so puzzled or give you 'odd' replies. You need to tune into what they understand at the moment.

Jacqui Cousins also gives useful pointers to valuable open-ended questions from adults: 'What made you say that?', 'why do you think that?', 'do you mean..?', 'I wonder what you were thinking then' and 'what made you ask that question?'

Four-year-olds can benefit from adult-initiated experiences that stretch the children's current knowledge – so long as adult plans connect well with what young children currently understand. Many aspects of their world are puzzling to young children and a careful and flexible topic or project approach can open those doors for new knowledge. However, the materials for the EYFS confirm what has always been the situation for the Foundation Stage. Flexible planning through topics is one way of looking ahead, to support children's learning in this or any other area of their development. But the method is not compulsory and nor does it work unless open-ended adult plans are very responsive – in timing, content and short-term final planning - to the actual interests of individual young children.

Learning in the outdoors

The New Zealand early childhood curriculum is called Te Whariki, a Maori phrase that means 'a woven mat on which all may stand'. One of the key strands within the curriculum is that of 'belonging'. Within this strand there is a goal that, 'children and their families experience an environment where connecting links with the family and the wider world are affirmed and extended'. One learning outcome within this goal is that 'children develop knowledge about the features of the area of physical and/or spiritual significance to the local community, such as the local river or mountain'.

In Maori cultural tradition, natural features of the landscape are sometimes of great cultural and religious significance. This learning outcome would not transplant neatly to the UK situation. But it is worth considering in what ways our early years settings could explore with four-, and five-year-olds what is of local significance and meaning. What might be equivalents for us?

The move to re-establish the outdoor curriculum, the forest school movement and outdoor projects like the Rising Sun Woodland Project (see page 67) show that children flourish when they are given experience to connect themselves to the outdoors, nature and the natural world. This emphasis on the outdoors is not only an issue for urban children. For instance, the Bridgwater Forest school is situated in what looks to a visitor like easily accessible countryside. But the team working with four-year-olds in the woodland resource realised that a high proportion of the children had scarcely visited the countryside that surrounds their town in Somerset.

Children learn outside as well as indoors and many four-year-olds are enthused by being outdoors. The learning area of Knowledge and Understanding of the World is impossible to envisage without easy access to an outdoor area and the interests of the local neighbourhood. When children are enthusiastic about and engaged in outdoor activity, they will promote their own learning in every aspect of development. (See also the discussion within 'Physical Development' on page 48.)

Answering the questions that children want to ask

The long example in this section shows the tracking of ideas over a year led by the thinking of one four-year-old. If you track the children in your setting, noting their questions and queries, in partnership with parents, you will find similar examples of the powerful thinking and curiosity of four-year-olds about the world around them.

For example

Four-year-olds ask a wide range of questions and the pattern will be an individual one. In the diary I kept of my son, Drew, I noted some diverse questions that he asked over the year that he was four years old. He was working to unravel some complex concepts and he returned to those on several occasions in his own chosen time frame. Drew appeared to be doing a lot of thinking, because he would return to some topics from a new or different angle weeks later. He asked direct questions, and made comments in a questioning tone of voice, to check whether he had got the right idea or not.

I learned over this year how important it was to answer each question as Drew asked it, to follow his lead if he had another question, but to avoid assuming what that question was likely to be. It was also important to stop within the conversation when he was finished for now. I learned my lesson fast from the couple of times I tried to carry on talking when his mind had headed off to the next point of interest. He would look sideways at me as if to communicate, 'surely we've finished', then carry on with his own, different line of discussion or simply wander off.

What is happening in the world and why?

- Drew had begun to watch the news on Newsround. The images he saw generated some of his questions about the wider world. He was concerned about the famine at that time and asked, 'why are the people hungry in Ethiopia?'
- Drew wanted to work out what was real and what was not and began to realise that some of what he could see on television was really happening and some was just a story. His concept, as reflected in his questions, became to ask what and who 'is in this world?'
- He wanted to know 'are there bombs in this world' and 'are there baddies in this world'. Sometimes he showed concern about what we could do about the fact that 'there are baddies in this world' and would they come after our family. He also became concerned about bombs, asking 'are bombs easy to make?' and then 'can we make bombs in our house?' I offered him reassurance but on one occasion did find myself announcing, 'Drew, I'm definitely not having a bomb in our house!'

The natural world

- He was very interested within the year about stars, planets and how astronomers could study the sky. His interest was supported by reference books that he was given for his own shelf or that he chose to get out of our local library. Drew had been interested to look at the 'moon and stars' since two years of age.
- Drew was also interested in the weather and how it came about. I did not have easy answers to many of his questions, like, 'why do you get a double rainbow' after we had seen this amazing sight one afternoon.

Bodies and growth

- Drew became interested in bodies and how they worked, stimulated partly by some illustrated information books about the human body. Drew wanted to know, 'how do you breathe?' and 'what would happen if we didn't have bones?' He was intrigued for some time with the pictures of the human skeleton and that this structure was inside all of us.
- Drew began several conversations over the year that circled around related issues of body size for children, age and what was fixed and what was not.

- He started with the question of, 'are my T-shirts getting small?' Since I knew I had not shrunk anything recently, I was able to say, 'no' and was about to ask, 'what makes you think that?' when Drew himself posed an alternative explanation, 'well, am I getting bigger then? Because Tanith's got my red T-shirt now.' A world in which clothes became smaller would explain the situation logically as well as children getting bigger, so your T-shirt then fitted your younger and smaller sister. But Drew had concluded that the growth explanation was more likely.
- Drew worked out you cannot overtake people in age. He would always be older than his sister Tanith. Matt, a child who was a year older, would always be older than Drew but, one day Drew might be as big or bigger than Matt.

Family relationships

- Within this year Drew met for the first time the part of our family that lives in the United States. He became interested in how everyone linked together and for a while liked to explore the connections in almost a quiz fashion. He would pose the questions of, 'who is Mummy's Mummy?' and 'who is Tracy's (his cousin) Daddy's Daddy?"
- He became able by talking out loud, often to work logically through the family relationships. He also discovered steadily by his questions that familiar people had different roles in the family network, for instance that I was 'Mummy' to him and Tanith, but also 'daughter' to his grandmother Nangi and 'sister' to Tracy's Daddy. Grandma Elsie was his Daddy's Mummy and Daddy had once been small, so maybe one day Drew would be as big as Daddy.
- Drew's conversational explorations about the family linked in with coming to grips with age as well. We had more than one conversation about the immediate family. Drew steadily worked out by question and questioning comment that he was born first, so he was older than his sister, Tanith. But being older was nothing to do with being a brother or sister. Drew grasped that you did not have to be older to be a brother. He needed to check this fact since Matt was also a firstborn with a younger sister. Drew was learning that, although boy followed by girl was the pattern in the two families he knew best, it was irrelevant to the sibling business. Drew recognised that he was a brother because he was a boy; being a boy was important, not being the older one.

Birth, babies, life and death

- Drew was interested as a young four-year-old in 'fat tummies', because this sight could mean a baby, if the person was a lady. He asked questions about just how tiny babies were when they started and how they got out of the Mummy's tummy. But it was several months before he asked questions about exactly how the babies got into a Mummy's tummy. I explained simply about eggs, sperms, Mummies and Daddies. I explained that sperms looked a bit like tadpoles but much, much smaller. I was ready to answer more questions, but this analogy led Drew into telling me about the tank with tadpoles in his nursery class and how sad it was that most of the tadpoles had died.
- Drew also approached the other end of life with questions about dying. His first question on this topic was not in fact 'the big one'. He asked, 'what happens when you die?' I was several sentences into what felt like an honest explanation, not too heavy on the philosophy, when Drew cut in with an impatient, 'no, no, no! I mean do you go like this?' He gave a good impression of a staggering and theatrical death and I said that dying was not usually this dramatic. Drew wandered off satisfied.
- Drew did not return to the topic of dying for a couple of months. He then asked about dying and said, 'but I won't die, will I?' His father answered honestly that everyone died at some point, but that Drew had many years to go. Drew was initially sceptical and then distressed that he would die. We reassured him that the most likely event was that he would live for many many years. A month or so later we were watching 'The Secret Garden' on television and

Being a helpful adult

- Make sure that computer ICT applications genuinely support learning for four-year-olds. Some language and maths packages have a narrow learning scope and children will practise the skills far more effectively with real materials.

- Some software offers limited scope for four-year-olds to consider why they are choosing one option over another; they learn instead to keep trying the choices until the programme tells them they are correct.

- Four-year-olds benefit from experiencing ICT, including computers, as part of play and practical tasks. Much like with reading and writing, children need to explore the why, what and how of computer usage.

- Settings support this message when the computer area is placed within the main space, rather than in a separate room. Four-year-olds need to see ICT as a source of tools, that work alongside the children's existing skills and knowledge.

reached the point where Colin calls out, 'I shall live forever!' Drew said seriously to me, 'but he won't. Everybody dies' and I explained that in the story Colin felt so much better from his ill health that he felt like the happiness would go on forever.

- A month or so later Drew asked the question, 'what happens when you die?', with the meaning I had wrongly assumed months earlier. Consistent with our family beliefs I said that, 'nobody knows for certain' and then gave simple alternatives that some people believed in a heaven after death and some people believed that we come back as a new baby and that was called reincarnation.

- Drew was very interested and took on board that everyone had 'different beliefs'. This concept proved useful when Jamie, from a Catholic family, told him that everyone who was not a Catholic (including our family) definitely went to hell when they died. Drew was distressed by the blunt prediction of doom. He cheered up when I explained that Jamie and his family held this belief, but it was just a belief and I believed just as strongly that it was not true.

Information and communication technology

It is important to recall that ICT is not only about computers (see also page 47 in *What Does it Mean to be Three?*) ICT covers the four-year-old interest in everyday technology, familiar from the home, like remote controls and videos, and seen in the local neighbourhood, such as pedestrian crossing signals, CCTV and check-outs at supermarkets.

Iram Siraj-Blatchford and John Siraj-Blatchford, have identified two important strands in placing ICT appropriately in the early years curriculum:

1. Helping children to develop an 'emergent technological literacy', including that they understand that there is wide usage of ICT.
2. Supporting children's practical skills to access and use the tools that ICT offer.

Four- and five-year-olds will not understand exactly how it all works in different types of ICT, but then neither do adults. The focus is on recognising the many forms of ICT in everyday life, including children's own home. In order to promote this learning, practitioners need to be aware and confident in the wide use of ICT. Sometimes it is a source of relief and confidence when early years teams realise that ICT is more than computers and includes technologies with which they are already familiar. It is important, however, that practitioners do grow in confidence in using all the basic tools, including those on computers. Parents may also be pleased to understand that ICT is a broader and perhaps more recognisable set of materials than computer software.

There are many ways in which four-year-olds show their skills and interest in ICT.

- Four-year-olds are interested in 'grown-up' technology that they can access through their play, frequently through their pretend play. They enjoy playing with pretend mobile phones but also appreciate using a proper phone or a walkie-talkie.

- It is now common in early years settings for children to have access to a camera, sometimes a disposable version. Four-year-olds show care and respect for what they recognise as 'grown-up' equipment. They learn technique, and can be given friendly advice. More settings now have a digital camera and children can be involved in taking pictures. But some fours are adept at working with images on the screen and knowledgeable about what their system will do. Even if adults are not yet at ease to hand over the digital camera, children can be fully involved in deciding what should be done with the images. I have now also encountered several settings (Buckingham's

Nursery being one of them), which have a lap top set up in the open area to the nursery with the current set of photos running as a display for parents.

- Four-year-olds are interested to look at high street technology and delighted if you can organise for a shop manager to show them how the check-out operates or the CCTV. Children often visit the local library on a regular basis and are interested in the scanner to check out books and perhaps the library database for tracking books
- In a family home, with their parents or childminder, four-year-olds like to help and are ready to learn about domestic technology such as the washing machine or dishwasher. In fact, it is safer to show them how such machines work, and explain any safety issues clearly, otherwise keen four-year-old helpers may try to operate the machine themselves. When our burglar alarm was fitted at home, we had children ranged from three to seven years of age utterly fascinated by the movement recorder. They spent a long time trying to crawl low and slow to get past the sensor without the light going on.
- In a family home, fours and younger children are interested in domestic appliances, like a cooker and washing machine, and how they work. Group settings, like nurseries are required to keep children out of the utility room. But teams, who recognise how much children learn, let them be involved in every aspect of the routine, except actually stepping into the room with the washing machine and drier.
- Four-year-olds can be dextrous and already apply their concentration and fine physical skills to work audio cassettes and video equipment, cameras, the computer keyboard and mouse or roller ball.

For example

Children learn from technology that can be used, perhaps initially with adult supervision.

- In the Grove Nursery School several children had been closely involved in a writing project linked to the hairdressers' role-play area that they wished to create. Children had discussed and helped to draft a letter for parents that explained their plans and made a request for a list of items to stock the hairdressers. They then used the nursery photocopier, with adult support, sorted out the letters and stood and handed them out to each parent at pick-up time.
- Also in the Grove, children had access to a fascinating technology table, covered in old telephones, cassette players and anything mechanical or technological (the batteries were removed) that was no longer wanted. The table was equipped with a proper screwdriver and some wire cutters and children were encouraged to take a look at what was inside some of these familiar items. On my visit I was genuinely intrigued as one four-year-old girl adeptly took apart a telephone and showed me what the insides looked like. I was able honestly to say that I had never seen the inside of a telephone before.
- In Windham Nursery School the children also knew that they could ask to use the photocopier, accompanied by an adult. The well resourced writing area – outdoors as well as inside, had a store of little whiteboards. Whenever children wanted a copy to keep of what they had drawn or written on their board, they just asked for a trip to the photocopier.
- A family had donated an old video player to Windham and, over the entire summer term, this equipment was left on a table and children took it apart bit by bit. When I visited towards the end of the term, the deconstruction was almost complete. Children were proud to show a visitor what they had done and discovered about the insides of a video player. They also fully understood, like the children in Grove, that you did not take a screwdriver and cutters to anything unless the adults had told you it was alright.

Physical Development

Four-year-olds' physical development is just as important as all the other areas of their learning. Four-year-olds need to be active for their physical, emotional and mental health. Many of the examples in this book show how children learn and concentrate while on the move. Indeed, being able to move is often a crucial part of four-year-old active learning.

Given a choice, four-year-olds go outdoors and many will spend most of their time in the garden or outdoor space. As many early years settings have discovered, it is possible to offer every aspect of the early years curriculum outside as well as inside. We need to put to rest the strange idea that children can only learn if they are sitting still indoors, and that brief bursts of outdoor time are just for 'letting off steam'.

Tight control of outdoor time tends to be a self-fulfilling prophecy. Four-year-olds, or other age groups who are desperate to get outdoors, will tend to rush round at speed, in an attempt to pack in all their favourite activities before they are made to return inside. Of course, outdoor play is not exclusively physical, but the two have become intermingled in unbalanced early years priorities. Children can gain in so many ways by easy access to their outdoor space:

- Children, who are enthused by projects, will talk together with energy. They engage in planning, raising ideas and problem-solving.
- Children learn, with wise adult support, to handle negotiation, turn taking and delegation.
- In their projects they make informed judgements, decisions and learn from the consequences of their experimentation with materials.
- The outdoor space allows larger scale projects such as creating a den, transporting material about the garden and spreading out with a project.
- There are greater opportunities in an outdoor space for being more energetic and louder, even when the garden is not substantial. Lively pretend play can expand in the outdoors.
- Children enjoy places to sit in comfort outside. They may wish to play together but children also often want to chat, with each other and with you.

Physical skills of four-year-olds

Discussion of physical development is often sub-divided into large movements (or gross motor development) and fine movements, often linked with co-ordination between hands and eyes. Yet this distinction is not meaningful in practice. Children need to pay close attention when they use their larger movements, and activities like climbing or bike riding need careful co-ordination and swift decision-making. The fine co-ordinations sometimes linked with the skills of learning to write do not operate in isolation. In fact, there are strong reasons for encouraging children in large movements that enable them to become confident in balance and bodily awareness. These skills are just as important for writing dexterity.

Four-year-olds are usually competent in a wide range of skills. They are physically competent, compared with their two- or three-year-old selves, but they still have much to learn and practise.

- Children are adept at running and four-year-olds usually have improved control over their movement, so that they can adjust their speed and direction most of the time.
- Part of physical development is the steady improvement in children's balance, their judgement of physical movements and their sense of bodily awareness. Four-year-olds who have practised balancing games and activities are often fairly confident at low wall walking and climbing.
- The application of four-year balancing skills depends on what is available. When they are given the opportunity, four- and five-year-olds can learn to ice skate or ski - activities often associated with much older children or adults.

In order to become confident, four-year-olds need plenty of practice in what it feels like to be in balance, to begin to lose your balance and sometimes regain it after a wobble. When adults are excessively concerned about children's safety and reducing accidents to an unrealistic zero, four-year-olds may not get enough experience to become confident.

- Children use their physical skills in games, pretend play and for sheer enjoyment. They show greater control of skills such as jumping, with some ability to judge landing, although not always with success and in using skills with equipment like a small trampoline.
- Physical skills are applied to riding three-wheeled bikes; some rising fives are close to the balance needed for two wheels without a stabiliser. Bike riding requires a combination of skills that are not always acknowledged by adults who dismiss the activity as 'just the bikes'. Four-year-olds need to practise the sequence of skills to work the pedals in a steady forward action and also to work out how to steer round other people or obstacle courses.

Children's physical movements require other related skills and bodily awareness. It can be easy for adults to underestimate the complexity of some physical sequences and how much children need to experience enjoyable practice.

- Four-year-olds can co-ordinate the handling, moving and lining up of equipment like ladders or blocks. They are able to work together on large-scale constructions like den building with other children or an adult. Although such activities may look like exclusively large physical movements, the tasks actually require delicate adjustments and bodily awareness.
- Children enjoy playing games with equipment like bats or balls. Such play combines careful looking, judgement of timing and aiming, as well as the physical actions of hitting, throwing or kicking. Learning to hit or kick a ball takes co-ordination and plenty of enjoyable practice. Even five- and six-year-olds are still learning some of these skills.

- Four-year-olds who have been given scope to practise and experiment can be skilled in the use of a wide range of tools, such as scissors, craft and woodwork equipment (see the examples on page 57). Tool use is supported by the intellectual skills of planning and recall, as well as the communication and negotiation skills required for cooperative working with friends.
- Four-year-olds' improved co-ordination shows in their increasing ability to share in their own care and help in daily routines at home and nursery.
- Some four-year-olds will now show a definite right or left hand preference, although some will still be flexible. There is no question that adults must respect the child's preference.

For example

In New River Green I was in the home corner with two children: Clement (four years old) and Rosie (three years). Clement moved across to a shelf on which a range of materials were easily accessible. He took a page of a magazine out of one basket. It was a complex maze to join together items on a sheet featuring Rice Krispies. Rosie suggested I use my pen but I was uncertain if that was all right, so I suggested that we should trace the wiggly lines with our finger.

Clement and Rosie both looked as if they enjoyed following the lines with their finger and explored between them most of the linkages. Clement started to explain to me what was featured on the sheet. Pointing to the images of special spoons he explained, 'they are in the bottom of the packet. You take out the packet and they are in the bottom'. The spoons are free gifts in packets of Rice Krispies but not every packet. Clement explained to me that one day, 'I brought a little Rice Krispies to nursery, but you don't get them (the spoons) in the little packets.'

Judging physical movements and safety

Many four-year-olds are fairly accurate in their judgements of climbing and jumping. Children are less able to make safe decisions in situations where they do not understand all the factors, such as crossing the road.

- Some four-year-olds are more cautious than others, and perhaps always will be. Some children need to take their time, just as others may benefit from a respectful, 'just take a look before you start'.

- By and large, four-year-olds are usually safe at judging what they can manage in physical skills. Problems tend to arise when they are distracted or pushed. They can also be distracted by constant cries of 'be careful! You'll fall!' from adults.

- Four-year-olds have considerably more awareness of their own body and ability to direct their movements in a deliberate way. Children have gained some awareness of the physical messages of their body when they make different actions. This awareness of physical feedback is called proprioception. The awareness can be the source of enjoyable physical games for four-year-olds, such as deliberately spinning around to make themselves dizzy or hanging upside down to see the world from that perspective.
- Four-year-olds make sense of some mathematical concepts through physical activity. For example, the feelings of moving fast or slow, being close to or a long way away and the directional awareness of forwards, backwards, up and down and round and round.

Health and bodily awareness

Much of children's understanding about bodies and bodily functions arises from conversations they want to have and questions they want to ask. Keeping clean enough and the reasons for hygiene can also develop through involvement of four year olds in their own daily routines, supported by simple explanations from adults. Children's interest in how bodies work shows how their desire to know supports the extension of their general knowledge. It is also a reminder that helpful adults need to work with what intrigued children enough today to want to ask their own questions.

Some discussions about bodies arise through ordinary daily events. Getting hot or cold is of meaning to four-year-olds and they learn about ways to keep well and healthy.

- In New River Green a practitioner approached one of the boys and asked, 'Harry, why is your face all red? Are you hot?' The boy nodded and the practitioner suggested, 'you know what might be a good idea? If you take your hat off.' The boy agreed and the adult took his hat saying, 'I'll put it on the shelf for you.'
- My visits to Buckingham's Nursery were spread over the summer and, it being England, some of the days were hot and some were cool and wet. I noticed many instances when practitioners reminded children, in a friendly way, about wearing their sun hat and offered help with the sun cream. On other days the adults took the time for a chat about what the weather was like and the question of 'do we need our coats today?'

Food and social mealtimes are of great significance to threes and fours. Consultations with young children have often found that they speak up, without being asked direct questions, with opinions about the food they like and happy memories about picnics in the garden. Children are far more likely to learn about food and healthy choices from genuine involvement in food preparation and meal organisation than rather disconnected projects about 'food' or 'our bodies'. Thoughtful early years teams, not only childminders, involve children in simple, real cooking, preceded if at all possible, by a shopping trip for ingredients. I have encountered nurseries, and a few primary schools as well, who have created a garden to grow vegetables or fruit with children. The crop has then been picked together, cleaned up and enjoyed in a meal. These kinds of experiences also support young learning for Knowledge and Understanding of the World and other aspects of their development.

Movement and transition

Children need to be physically active – indeed the early years are crucial time to lay down this particular healthy habit. Children should not be expected to sit for long stretches in their day or session. But they do need help to sit sometimes.

For example

The Windham nursery school team have created a well-resourced indoor and outdoor learning environment and the children are able to move around easily. There is much careful adult planning, but it is discreet. The planning shows itself through resources, adult-initiated activities offered with choice and practitioners who are playful and conversational. The pattern of the day is that there is a coming together time at the end of the morning and afternoon. The team have put thought into how to manage this transition from freely chosen play to the one time when children are asked to be in a whole group. I visited towards the end of the summer term but even the older fours still needed the caring support offered by this thoughtful routine.

- Children are eased, with warning, from self-chosen play towards tidying up: a making things tidy process at the end of the morning and full tidy-up at the end of the afternoon. The children are fully involved in this active work.
- The tidy-up time is followed by physical games in small groups that adults lead in the outdoor area: traditional games like 'Oranges and Lemons'.
- The routine moves towards sitting in one area of the indoors space for children to have their fruit, with the helpers of the day being the only children on the move.
- Practitioners touch children gently on the head to move five or six at a time from the fruit circle to the informal rows for singing. There is then a short and active singing time as a group.
- All the practitioners are involved, so any individual children who find the

transition more difficult to manage can be guided by an adult sitting close to them.

- The team use specific short songs to ease children from movement to listening. Part of the singing time is also using sound makers to shake and tap in a rhythm that includes a stop phase: being still as well as active.
- The children enjoy a small number of songs, all of which include actions. There is the opportunity for a few children each time to join two practitioners at the front of the group to do the appropriate actions with props.

The Windham team placed an importance on routine. They took the view that young children benefit from routine that is predictable but not rigid. I agree that all young children like to know what will happen within their day, whether they are in nursery, with their childminder or in their own home. Then, children younger than the fours begin to anticipate what will happen next and start to operate in an appropriately independent way.

Young children, right up to and including the early years of school, need to feel at ease within their daily routine. When children are sure of routines, they feel confident to organise themselves more – a skill that children need as they enter their school years. In contrast, children are anxious when adults do not take time and trouble to manage their expectations and create predictability in the day. Children then spend precious emotional energy searching for clues about what happens next, wondering 'is this what I'm supposed to be doing?' 'What do the adults want this time?'

Creative Development

Young children have a fresh outlook on life that sets them up well for creativity. Fours are very open to possibilities and have an enthusiasm for using ideas and materials in whatever way works. Creative development can be supported by child-friendly arts and crafts but creativity also flourishes through imagination and the buzz of independent thought. Creativity is closely connected with all the other areas of development.

An environment to encourage creativity

Linda Thornton and Pat Brunton describe how early years settings in the Italian city Reggio Emilia work with an approach that gives a central importance to children's learning through the expressive arts. The teams do not ignore literacy or numeracy activities; it is rather that they observe how children learn through a wide range of creative forms.

They emphasise giving the time to explore projects of genuine interest to the children. This approach is consistent with the 'hundred languages' vision of Loris Malaguzzi, a teacher whose ideas were central to how the Reggio early educational system developed. The key issues are directly relevant to how we support children's learning in the UK and good practice reflects a version of this kind of approach:

- Four-year-olds, and younger or slightly older children, cannot express themselves if their explorations are firmly bounded by adult definitions of time and space: how long a project should take, where it should happen and what defines 'finished' and 'good enough'.

- The Reggio approach takes seriously what was also long regarded as good early years practice in the UK: that the process of undertaking a project is what enables children to learn and to be genuinely creative in expression.
- The end product matters, as the behaviour of young children will often show. But product cannot be allowed to overshadow process, especially if that product risks being pre-determined by adult plans and standards.

Creativity and imagination

Four-year-olds are able to be very expressive and to communicate through verbal and non-verbal means.

- Children apply their skills and imagination in their own chosen use of dance, music or different forms of sound making.
- Four-year-olds can show great pleasure in singing, both in group singing times and through choice in spontaneous singing and sound making.
- Children show imagination in how they explore, tell and begin to act out parts of a story.

For example

At New River Green it was tidying-up time before lunch. The children gathered in one part of the nursery space and the tidying tasks were shared out. Children went off to different corners of the room and set about their tasks. I stayed with the three children who were tidying up in the home corner. They were busy chatting as they tidied up, and were capable of chatting and tidying efficiently at the same time. Clement (four years old) said with excitement, 'we're going to have some lunch today!' A second child repeated the phrase and they spontaneously made it into a song, like a refrain. The three children sang, 'I need some lunch, we're having some lunch, we always have some lunch' and they repeated the 'verses' several times very tunefully, as they continued with their tidying task.

This example shows children's ability to concentrate and do more than one thing at the same time, especially when they have a clear practical task in a familiar context and they are motivated to complete it.

I think the sequence also shows how young children, who feel happy, will break into spontaneous song. In this way, singing can well be viewed as an indicator of emotional well-being.

Four-year-olds often show immense creativity through rich pretend play. Using minimal props, four-year-olds explore many different play themes and with a regular friendship group will return to those themes day after day. Observant practitioners can often offer ideas and some themes, chosen by children, may turn into a semi-permanent role-play area.

Four-year-olds show thinking and planning, language skills and recall as they direct play themes themselves, decide on characters, negotiate the 'scripts' and plan out the action to a certain extent. Vivian Gussin Paley's observations have shown that feelings can run high when concerns and worries from outside the setting are imported into play by young children. Children work through a wide range of experiences in play and the task of early years practitioners is to create a positive emotional environment in which this exploration is safe.

Being a helpful adult

Early years practitioners do well to reflect on what is creativity, what supports creative expression and what blocks it.

- An activity is not genuinely creative just because adults label it as such.
- If you have very structured activities, in which children are directed to make a picture or a model 'like this', then children will learn to follow directions and judge themselves against the 'right one'.
- But children also need constructive feedback and friendly help with technique in use of tools and materials.
- Children become frustrated if they are left to reinvent the wheel when there are more effective ways to use a saw or a needle (see the example on page 57).
- It also helps four-year-olds to understand that everyone gets better with practice. Adults were not born knowing how to hammer, wield a paintbrush or make towers that do not collapse.
- Children are more engaged if they have been involved in choice and direction of any topics and themes. Reflective adults need to consider why has this 'creative' activity been introduced? What has come from the children in this choice? If nothing at all, then do not be surprised if an activity does not work that well.

For example

I enjoyed listening and watching a long pretend play sequence in the block area of New River Green Centre between Rosie (three years) and Ben (four years), who spent quite a lot of time together at different parts of the day.

The entire sequence lasted for close to half an hour and the two young children moved seamlessly from one theme to another. Two adults were close by: an early year practitioner sitting at a nearby table, sometimes with other children and Ben's mother who was staying in response to his request that she play with him a while before she left. The example is described in detail in *What Does it Mean to be Three?* (page 60), but some highlights are given here:

- Ben and Rosie used blocks and wooden planks to build a see-saw structure and then a bridge.
- Their comments to each other and the adults demonstrated how they were using their eyes to judge what was needed and had a grasp of positional concepts.
- At various times in their relaxed and spontaneous play, Rosie and Ben explored rockets and bridges.
- They defended their space against fierce dragons, and then dinosaurs.
- Later they draped their wooden constructions with material and created an impromptu lunch.

Children's creativity in pretend play has been limited potentially by a ground rule that has been common for many years in early years settings. It became usual for teams to bring to a halt any pretend play that included what adults judged to be war and weapons play on the rationale that such play was aggressive. In many settings, the limits extended to any superhero or monster themes that thrilled many children, especially boys.

Penny Holland worked with a North London nursery to try a change in policy, because of the concerns in the team about the impact on children, who became creative and secretive as they continued imaginative play of their own choice. Parents were informed by a letter, but otherwise the ban on superhero and weapons play was lifted without any special announcement to the children. The experience of this nursery, documented by Penny Holland, reflects what has happened elsewhere with thoughtful teams.

For a short period of time, there was an increase in children's playing the previously forbidden games, especially involving weaponry. But once children realised that adults had ceased to halt this imaginary theme, the play extended, without aggressive content, into other forms of creative expression by word and drawings. Pretend play became longer and other children, including girls, were drawn into the imaginative and complex themes of play that lasted.

A similar process has been followed in New River Green. For example, the practitioner was able to observe Rosie and Ben's theme about defending their structure against the dragons. The children briefly held pieces of wood as imaginary weapons. But the play remained calm and there was no intervention by the adult.

Tools, technique and learning about safety

Four-year-old creativity in art, craft and activities like gardening can co-exist with safe use of tools and an understanding of hygiene. Children need to be taught technique as appropriate and safety within a practical context. They then need proper woodwork or craft tools that enable children to work on a satisfying project. So-called 'children's versions' in plastic not only do not do the job, but are more likely to split and break.

Early years practitioners, along with school and out-of-school teams, have to deal with safety concerns in ways that do not block children's learning or lead to a boring environment for children.

For example

On my visit to Grandpont Nursery in Oxford, it was possible to see how the four-year-olds used proper tools when they worked in their garden.

- The staff coached careful behaviour through conversation and demonstration, rather than any nagging.
- The head explained how the children themselves were able to explain safe use of the garden rakes with, 'We never let the rake come up higher than this' (upper body).
- This ground rule also then made sense to the children in how to handle their hockey sticks for a game.

Like many nursery teams who offer woodwork, Grandpont Nursery School found that, if parents were going to be uneasy about any nursery activity, it was more likely to be about the prospect of the woodwork table.

- The children learn to use proper hammers, pliers, a hand drill, saws, nails and sandpaper. The team takes time to meet parents' concerns with respect and explain how they coach in technique. For instance, children are shown carefully how to use the tools and they can start with soft wood before progressing to the harder pieces.
- Handy techniques are shared, such as holding a nail with pliers and then hammering it.
- In common with other nurseries I have encountered, who include woodwork experience, no child at the woodwork table in Grandpont has ever had more than an ordinary scrape or minor graze.

The Bridgwater Forest School team has faced and resolved similar issues:

- During their forest school sessions the four-year-olds from Bridgwater Children's Centre are shown how to use knives, saws and tenon saws. They learn these skills over the months of their year of visits, understanding the best techniques and following the few safety rules.
- One ground rule in the woodland is that only adults carry the tenon saws from place to place.

Being a helpful adult

Jo Goodall, in her presentations about supporting creativity, describes how simple materials and open-ended questions can promote creative thinking and actions. She uses materials in imaginative ways:

- Jo Goodall shows children two types of brick: one standard and one with three small circular holes. She then asks young children for their ideas about the possible uses of each brick. There are no right answers, of course.
- She provides a bag of hats, that children can choose and try on their head. Young children are able to imagine who is the person who wears this hat and what goes on around them.
- She also has a big collection of all different kinds of lids, including stoppers. Hands-on exploration helps children think and speculate about the direction of turning a lid, shape and fit, as well as the intriguing variety in something that appears as basic as a lid.
- In her work with children, Jo Goodall stresses what she calls the Rs: qualities such as resourceful, reflective, responsible, reliable and relating.

- The forest school team also places a high value on good communication with parents, with explanations, plenty of information and an invitation to join a camp at the end of their child's year of regular visits.

When children can access materials and friendly adult support, it is possible to see how their creative development links with other areas of their learning. The description of the woodwork table at New River Green highlights how the children were using physical skills, looking and listening, planning ahead and taking on useful tips for technique and safety.

For example

At New River Green, several children, aged three and four years, were concentrating well at the woodwork table that was set up on the covered veranda. Children were sawing through their own pieces of wood that they had selected from the wood store. Two practitioners were close by, watching and listening, and offered advice when appropriate or requested.

- The practitioners guided children without imposing their views and in ways that increased the chances that these three- and four-year-olds could feel satisfied. For instance, a practitioner commented on the size of wood to select and saw with, 'that one's too thick. It will take a very long time to saw'.
- There are more effective ways to use tools, not just related to safety, and it is unhelpful of adults to let children persevere in less effective techniques of tool use. Friendly advice was given and shown on sawing technique, with simple words and indicating some practical advice, such as 'you need to put the saw in the groove you've made', 'it's good to look at what you're doing' and 'that's it. Up and down strokes'.
- Sometimes one practitioner helped a child to line up the saw. The adults also ensured that the wood was firmly clamped to the table edge. The practitioners took responsibility for doing the actual clamping but by words and actions showed the children what they were doing and the reason - to hold a child's chosen piece of wood secure so the child could focus on the sawing.
- It took some time to saw all the way through the sections of wood but the children all focused and kept going, with the odd breather, until they had sawn off their own section. If they then wanted to take a break, their piece of wood was labelled with their name and put safe on a shelf, so they could come back to their work later.
- Some children chose to continue with their project. They could paint their wood and nail on other shapes, as they wished. Hammering in the nails was done on the second table nearby. A practitioner was sat at this table and offered advice but, as with the sawing, did not impose her views in any way.
- Any safety messages were given in a practical tone, with an explanation. At one point the practitioner showed a child how the nail had come through the other side of the two pieces of wood that she had fixed together. The end of the nail now stuck out, but the practitioner simply called the child's attention to this fact. The child then turned her wood over and hammered the end of the nail over, so it was now flat against her wood.
- The whole activity was relaxed. Three- and four-year-olds showed impressive concentration. It takes time to saw through a piece of wood, even the relatively small sections on which they worked - about a centimetre thick and 15 cm wide. But the children focused, even at the tough stage of getting the first sawing groove established. Other children watched with interest, chatted and waited their turn patiently.
- The children were able to take their time with the practical task and with choices. The adults watched, showing genuine interest (not vague supervision), kept the children company,

offered low-key practical advice and admired what children had accomplished. Some children were in mid-project when it was time to stop for lunch. They were able to put their work in progress in their basket or on the shelf, so they could return to it in the afternoon.

Creative expression and child-led projects

Adults cannot 'make' young children be creative. Creativity develops from open-ended situations in which children have good resources of material and an adult who will follow their lead, adding but not directing what unfolds. As with many other activities with young children, too much questioning from adults actually derails the creative process and any outcome. Early settings sometimes have the opportunities provided by an artist in residence. So long as that person is also attuned to young children, some absorbing and long-running projects can result. Young children sometimes have their own projects in mind, perhaps led by a need like, 'somewhere comfy to sit outside' or 'a nice shelter when it's very sunny or windy'. Look at the creative ideas described in the Curiosity and Imagination resource (see page 65 for full reference). This set of twelve projects shows very clearly that genuine creativity takes time and space. An absorbing project can start with ideas from an adult, from the children and a combination of both. The crucial good practice point for supporting young learning is that children have genuine input in the development of the long-term project.

Some large scale projects flourish in the space of the outdoors and some natural materials offer great scope for outdoor art and sculpture. I am grateful to Diane Rich, who first made me aware of the work of the English artist, Andy Goldsworthy. You can see a wide range of his creations on www.goldsworthy.cc.gla.ac.uk/browse/ Children often relate well to the wonder of the outdoors and are thrilled to see what they can choose to create with sticks, leaves, stones and all the natural materials that are outdoors for free.

For example

In Bridgwater Children's Centre all the children have easy access to an outdoor space with many corners and sections. It is easy for children to organise natural materials in ways that they want and practitioners are very flexible about the outdoors literally being brought indoors. On two visits, I watched children who were busy laying out materials as they wanted, which in some cases involved a pleasing array of sticks and branches.

Those early years settings who value outdoor learning give children generous access to the garden. The growing Forest School and outdoors movement has shown the rich learning opportunities that open up for children when they have access to their own outdoor space or a special woodland for visits. Children learn directly about the natural world - knowledge and understanding of the world - and, they learn to use tools in a safe and effective way. Additionally, over time, children can pursue creative problem solving.

The team at Sightlines Initiative are committed to outdoor learning and to the insights from the Reggio approach to early learning. Their visual record of the Rising Sun Woodland project (see page 67 for details) shows very effectively how a group of three- and four-year-olds learned to move within a woodland space. The footage, taken over many months, also shows very effectively how all six areas of development evolve for young children in a connected way, through experiences that matter to them.

- The children had direct hands-on and wellingtons-on experience of the natural world and the changing seasons. They developed practical projects that had meaning and which lasted over time, because the children were enthused. They had reasons for wanting to measure the depth and width of the pond or how to ensure that the newly planted bulbs would not get trampled.
- The children had a long-term interest in the pond, which was the one part of the woodland area that always had an adult close by. The changing state of the pond over the seasons of the year was of continued interest to the children: full coverage of water in one large pond, iced over water in winter, shrinking of the pond so that it became two ponds and then dried up altogether. Children wanted to assess the depth of the pond when it was full of water, explore with glee the muddy surrounds and speculate on where the water had gone in the summer.
- The nursery and woodland team shared the philosophy that the children would drive their own learning; there were no adult determined projects. The children themselves determined what they would do, so the morning and afternoon groups followed some different patterns. Children wanted to use the resources of the woodland to make structures: some parts for their dragon, nest making, dens and a wooden man/monster.
- The children collected 'treasures' - all different kinds of natural materials - and their glee in activities like mud splashing led to some creative ideas about ways to classify different types of mud.
- The children learned tool use in a practical context, with proper tools that worked and adults to help as necessary. Like the Bridgwater Forest School, the Rising Sun project took the opportunity to introduce children to fire and to support safety learning in this real context. The building of the bonfire emerged again from a practical issue, that it was cold and wet and 'how do we get dry and warm?'

Creativity and aesthetic appreciation

Four-year-olds develop in technical skills but also in the personal satisfaction that develops from being able to make choices of technique, materials, style and end product, or no end product at all. In some teams, the most important priority is that the adults address, and put to one side, their sense of pressure that children must produce something on a regular basis. The pressure particularly undermines creativity if there is a sense that all children must produce something similar.

Children are undoubtedly very pleased to see their work in pride of place, but they need to be able to make their own decisions about what they make and when they have finished. It can help if adults reflect on their own attitudes to the wall space.

- The team at Windham Nursery School (see also page 14) significantly reduced the number of display boards in their setting. On reflection they felt that big areas of wall space of this kind simply put pressure on adults to get children to make paintings, collages and do project work that could be saved. It is so easy for adults to feel 'we must cover the wall'. If children do something that they want displayed, then of course there is this opportunity.
- Display does not have to mean flat wall space; some models or works in progress need shelf space.
- Some large projects can be 'kept' in the end by letting the children take photographs. Increasing numbers of early years settings now have a camera or more than one. Disposable cameras can meet adult anxiety about damage to expensive equipment. However, I have yet to encounter an early years settings where children have dropped or otherwise failed to take care of the camera.

For example

Four-year-olds who are allowed to explore and follow through their chosen projects can show creative problem-solving, experimentation and working together.

- When I visited Grandpont Nursery School in Oxford a small group of children had designed and built a channel to bring water over some distance from the outdoor tap to their sand pit. Lengths of firm plastic guttering had been supported by milk crates along its length and the system was working well. The construction was now complete and I asked the nursery head how it had evolved. She explained that the children had worked out their plan and put it into action entirely without adult suggestion or intervention. In this nursery the children had easy access in the garden to a wide range of materials and they could choose and transport using their own initiative.
- Safety issues had been discussed with all the children at an earlier stage, for instance about a height limit to construction using the milk crates. The children had listened to adult explanations that, 'we don't climb on the crates if they are more than two high, because it's very wobbly, like this...' The nursery head explained how she had heard children discuss the height limit and decide on options like, 'if we want to climb on them, we'll make it long and not high'.

I enjoyed watching a mixed group of twos, threes and fours in St Mark's Nursery School. The children relished having buckets of water and paintbrushes in the garden on a warm summer's day. The children were given a free choice about how to use the materials and had been very involved in the organisation of this opportunity.

- The younger children were fascinated by simple brushing onto the paved surface. They seemed to be interested in how the water disappeared in the heat of the day. The slightly older children experimented with the chalks that were also available. Some of them chose to chalk around the water then watched as the wet area retreated and shrunk. Their chalked outline was a clear indication of how far the wet area had dried out. These threes and fours had developed their own knowledge and understanding of a familiar world.
- The flexibility of materials in the nursery's outdoor area meant that the two-year-olds, the youngest in this setting, were able to make easy choices. So there was no need to have equipment especially for them. At least one painting easel and water tray were outside. During the same afternoon, two girls had organised their own outdoor book area under a large sunshade. They were able to lay out cloths and bring out books in a manageable container, because all these materials were available.

What should concern you?

Four-year-olds are a diverse group and individual temperament will vary, but some children will be a source of concern:

- Children who seem to have a fragile sense of self-esteem, who appear to be uncertain of their own worth. Perhaps they are concerned to get anything 'right' or have already taken on board a belief that they 'cannot' do something or are 'no use' at a whole area of skills.
- Children vary in social experience and the application of social skills. All children need to settle into a setting and deserve kindness and consideration from the adults, as they get used to your routines and ground rules. However, children who seem deeply perplexed about social interaction may have developmental disabilities within autistic spectrum disorder.
- Some children may need to be encouraged to relax and explore. Perhaps they have learned that children should answer adults' testing questions. Maybe children believe that difficulties in replying are their fault rather than an inability of adults to help children's confusion. Such an outlook will not be helped if children have been drilled in areas like early maths and do not understand the concepts through meaningful and ordinary applications.
- When children's spoken language or their understanding seems delayed for their age. There may be a number of reasons for children's difficulties: undiagnosed hearing problems, limited experience, learning disabilities and language disorders. Any steps must be taken in partnership with parents, but children are poorly served by any delay in getting help.
- Four-year-olds who have been put under pressure to learn to read or write before they were ready. Children who have been pressurised into doing 'proper' writing can not only be anxious but start developing physical problems from a cramped-up position and inappropriate pencil grip.
- Four-year-olds are usually interested and curious. It would be a source for concern if children were disinterested or cynical, although of course, children can be disengaged because the adults' approach is developmentally inappropriate or genuinely boring.
- Computers and other forms of ICT can have a positive part to play in learning. However, some four-year-olds have been allowed to spend excessive amounts of time on the computer already. It would be right to be concerned since hours spent at the computer screen will mean that children are far less engaged in other activities, such as physically active games, conversation or creative projects.
- Four-year-olds will not have perfect balance and some co-ordinations are still challenging for them, but you would be right to be concerned if children are experiencing persistent difficulties with physical skills of basic self-care, or a child had many accidents and slips that did not seem explicable by the circumstances.
- Four-year-olds can be competent but the experience of some boys or girls may have built the expectation that other people will perform most of their self-care. Steady

encouragement and adult support may be needed to build confidence and pleasure in competence.

- You need to be concerned and talk with parents about any difficulties that raise issues about children's confidence in their physical skills or their ability to engage in close observation. Hearing and vision may be of concern. Partial or variable problems in hearing or sight have not always been identified by four years of age.

Further Resources

Accessing materials about the Early Years Foundation Stage (EYFS)

The EYFS applies to England, will be statutory (under the Childcare Act 2006) and must be fully implemented from September 2008.

- At that point the EYFS will replace both Birth to Three Matters (currently for under threes) and the Foundation Stage (currently three- to five-year-olds) to create a birth to five years early childhood framework that, as was the case with the Foundation Stage, definitely includes children in reception class.
- From September 2008 the Welfare Requirements will replace the set of separate booklets of the National Care Standards. Inspection will be under sections 49 and 50 of the Childcare Act 2006.

The EYFS materials are mainly provided within a pack entitled *The Early Years Foundation Stage – Setting the Standards for Learning, Development and Care for children from birth to five*. This pack includes:

- Two booklets: the Statutory Framework and the Practice Guidance.
- The single set of Welfare Requirements are in the Statutory booklet.
- The Practice booklet includes the birth to five years descriptive developmental material and suggestions for good practice.
- A poster about the EYFS – led through the four broad, guiding themes of A Unique Child, Positive Relationships, Enabling Environments and Learning and Development.
- A set of twenty-four Principles into Practice cards, which provide key ideas and examples about good practice. The Statutory booklet makes it clear that these materials are central for guiding good practice.
- A CD Rom, which includes all the main materials. This resource also provides briefing papers, website links and a series of brief video excerpts.

All EYFS materials can be ordered from DCSF Publications tel: 0845 60 222 60 -reference number 00012-2007PCK-EN. Materials are also on: www.teachernet.gov.uk/teachingandlearning/EYFS www.standards.dfes.gov.uk/EYFS

The EYFS Briefing Pack for local authorities includes materials to guide training about the birth to five framework. Much of this resource is also useful to group leaders/managers and to childminders. The reference number is 00106-2007BKT-EN. These materials are also on the Teachernet website – look down the left-hand side on the EYFS home page.

Revised editions of the EYFS booklets were published in May 2008, and placed on the Teachernet website. This site has a list of the changes and a Q& A section.

Books and websites

- Bromley, Helen *Making My Own Mark: Play and Writing* (Early Education, 2006)
- Caddell, Dorothy *Numeracy Counts* (Scottish Consultative Council on the Curriculum 1998, can be downloaded from www.ltscotland.org.uk/earlyyears/Images/numeracycounts_tcm4-124480.pdf)
- Caddell, Dorothy *Numeracy in the Early Years: What the Research Tell Us* (Scottish Consultative Council on the Curriculum 1998, can be downloaded from www.ltscotland.org.uk/earlyyears/images/numeracyinearlyyears_tcm4-124469.pdf)
- Campbell, Robin *Literacy from Home to School: Reading with Alice* (Trentham Books 1999)
- Chilvers, Di *Young Children Talking: The Art of Conversation and Why Children Need to Chatter* (Early Education 2006)
- Clark, Alison and Moss, Peter *Listening to Young Children: The Mosaic Approach* (National Children's Bureau 2001)
- Cousins, Jacqui *Listening to Four Year Olds: How They Can Help Us Plan Their Education and Care* (National Children's Bureau 2003)
- Curiosity and Imagination (a project based at 4Children) *Inspiring Creativity and Imagination* 2005 - projects with children in early years centres download www.surestart.gov.uk/communications/childcareworkers/inspiringcreativity
- Daycare Trust *Listening to Children - Young Children's Views On Childcare: A Guide for Parents* (Daycare Trust 1998)
- Department of Education Northern Ireland – information about developments on www.deni.gov.uk
- Donaldson, Margaret *Children's Minds* (Fontana 1978 – for discussion in a more recently published book see Lindon, 2005)
- Dowling, Marion *Supporting Young Children's Sustained Shared Thinking: An Exploration* (DVD and booklet, Early Education 2005, tel: 020 7539 5400 www.early-education.org.uk)
- Duffy, Bernadette *Supporting Creativity and Imagination in the Early Years* (Open University Press 1998)
- EPPE: The Effective Provision of Pre-School Education project - a wide range of papers on www.ioe.ac.uk/schools/ecpe/eppe
- Fajerman, Lina; Jarrett Michael and Sutton Faye *Children as Partners in Planning: A Training Resource to Support Consultation with Children* (Save the Children 2000)
- Featherstone, Sally (ed) *L is for Sheep: Getting Ready for Phonics* (Featherstone Education 2006 www.featherstone.com.uk)
- Healy, Jane Your *Child's Growing Mind: Brain Development and Learning from Birth to Adolescence* (Broadway 2004)
- Holland, Penny *We don't Play with Guns Here: War, Weapon and Superhero Play in the Early Years* (Open University Press, 2003)
- Hughes, Anne and Ellis, Sue *Writing it Right? Children Writing 3-8* (Scottish Consultative Council on the Curriculum 1998, can be downloaded from www.ltscotland.org.uk/earlyyears/Images/writingitright_tcm4-124463.pdf)
- Hughes, Martin *Children and Number* (Blackwell, 1986)
- Learning and Teaching Scotland has an early years section on www.ltscotland.org.uk/earlyyears/ and publications that can be downloaded listed on www.ltscotland.org.uk/search/index.asp
- Kinney, Linda and McCabe, Jerry *Children as Partners: A Guide to Consulting with Very Young Children* (Stirling Council 2000 Tel: 01786 471177)

- Lewisham Early Years Advice and Resource Network *A Place to Learn: Developing a Stimulating Environment* (LEARN 2002 Tel: 020 8695 9806)
- Lindon, Jennie *Understanding Children's Play* (Nelson Thornes 2001)
- Lindon, Jennie *Too Safe for Their Own Good? Helping Children Learn about Risk and Life Skills* (National Children's Bureau 2003)
- Lindon, Jennie *Understanding Child Development: Linking Theory and Practice* (Hodder Arnold 2005)
- Lindon, Jennie *Equality in Early Childhood: Linking Theory and Practice* (Hodder Arnold 2006)
- Lindon, Jennie *Care and Caring Matter: Young Children Learning Through Care* (Early Education 2006)
- Lindon, Jennie *Safeguarding Children and Young People: Child Protection 0-18 years* (Hodder Arnold 2008)
- Locke, Ann and Ginsborg, Jane *Spoken Language in the Early Years: The Cognitive and Linguistic Development of Three- to Five-Year-Old Children from Socio-Economically Deprived Backgrounds* Educational and Child Psychology volume 20, 2003. See also the article *Catching Up or Falling Behind?* on www.literacytrust.org.uk/Pubs/ginsborg.html
- Marsden, Liz and Woodbridge, Jenny *Looking Closely at Learning and Teaching… A Journey of Development* (Early Excellence 2005)
- Miller, Judy *Never Too Young: How Young Children Can Take Responsibility and Make Decisions - A Handbook for Early Years Workers* (Save the Children, 2003)
- Munn, Penny 'What do children know about reading before they go to school?' in Owen, Pamela and Pumfrey, Peter (eds) *Emergent and Developing Reading: Messages for Teachers* (Falmer Press 1997)

- Munn, Penny 'Children's beliefs about counting' in Thompson, Ian (ed) *Teaching and Learning Early Numbers* (Open University Press, 1997)
- Nutbrown, Cathy; Hannon, Peter and Morgan, Anne *Early Literacy Work with Families: Policy, Practice and Research* (2005 Sage)
- Paley, Vivian Gussin *A Child's Work: The Importance of Fantasy Play* (University of Chicago Press, 2004)
- Palmer, Sue and Bayley, Ros *Foundations of Literacy: A Balanced Approach to Language, Listening and Literacy Skills in the Early Years* (Network Educational Press 2004)
- REPEY project *Researching Effective Pedagogy in Early Years: Brief No 356*: www.dfes.gov.uk/research/data/uploadfiles/RB356.doc
- Rich, Diane et al *First Hand Experiences: What Matters to Children* (2005 tel: 01473 737405 www.richlearningopportunities.co.uk)
- Siraj-Blatchford, Iram and Siraj-Blatchford, John *More Than Computers: Information and Communication Technology in the Early Years* (Early EducatioN 2003)
- Tizard, Barbara and Hughes, Martin *Young Children Learning* (Blackwell 2002)
- Thornton, Linda and Brunton, Pat *Bringing the Reggio Approach to Your Early Years Practice* (David Fulton 2007)
- Welsh Assembly - for information about the Foundation Phase in Wales http://new.wales.gov.uk/topics/educationandskills/policy_strategy_and_planning/earlywales/foundation_phase/foundation_phase_documents/?lang=en

Videos/DVDs

Check the relevant organisation for current prices. The only free resources are from Sure Start, Department of Children Schools and Families and Community Playthings.

- Community Playthings *The Value of Unit Block Play* one of many videos/DVDs from this source tel: 0800 387 457 www.CommunityPlaythings.co.uk
- High/Scope UK *Supporting Children in Resolving Conflicts* (tel: 020 8676 0220 www.high-scope.org.uk)
- National Children's Bureau *Tuning into Children* (Book and video tel: 020 7843 6000)
- Persona Dolls in Action (tel: 020 8446 7951 www.persona-doll-training.org)
- Sightlines Initiative *Rising Sun Woodland Pre-school Project* (Visual and written materials tel: 0191 261 7666 www.sightlines-initiative.com)
- Siren Film and Video Ltd *Attachment in Practice, Exploratory Play* and other learning and play titles from this source, tel: 0191 232 7900 www.sirenfilms.co.uk
- Sheffield University *REAL Project Early Literacy Education with Parents: A Framework for Practice* (Tel: 0114 222 0400)
- Sure Start – *Foundation Stage Toolkit* set of DVDs includes *Celebrating young children*. (Reference number DfES 1198-2005 GCDI, from the DCSF publications centre tel: 0845 6022 260.)

I have learned a great deal through discussions with early years practitioners and consultants and through visits to a wide range of early years settings. In connection with this book, I would especially like to thank the staff team and children at the following settings:

- Bridgwater Children's Centre and Forest School, Somerset
- Burnwood Nursery School, Staffordshire
- Grandpoint Nursery School, Oxford
- New River Green Early Years Centre and Family Project, North London (referred to in brief as New River Green)
- Saplings nursery, South London
- Soho Family Centre, Central London
- St Mark's Square Nursery School, North London
- St Peter's Eaton Square CE Primary School Nursery Class, central London (referred to in brief as St Peter's)
- The Grove Nursery School, South London
- Windham Nursery School, South London

With thanks to all the staff and children at Buckingham's Nursery School in Leek, Staffordshire Moorlands for making me so welcome during my consultancy with the nursery and for giving permission for me to use some of my observations in this book. The setting offers full day care for an age range from babies up to four-year-olds. In the examples I have referred to the group as Buckingham's Nursery.

I would like to thank the following individuals whose ideas on early years practice have been so valuable – and whose working role at the time is given in brackets:

- Jean Ainsworth-Smith (Head of St Peter's Eaton Square CE Primary School Nursery Class)
- Cherry Baker (Deputy Head of Windham Nursery within Windham Early Excellence Centre)
- Jacqui Cousins (Early Years Consultant)
- Louise Davies (Town and Country Kiddies, Louth)
- Annie Davy (Oxford EYDCP)
- Esther Hotherall (Head of the Grove Nursery School)
- Jo Goodall (Early Years Inspector at Walsall Education/Serco)
- Anita Mohindra (Head of New River Green Early Years Centre and Family Project)
- Penny Munn and her colleagues at the University of Strathclyde
- Diane Rich (Early Years Consultant)
- Iram Siraj-Blatchford (Professor of Early Childhood Education, Institute of Education)
- Penny Tassoni (Early Years Consultant)

I have changed the names of any children from examples observed in actual settings. Drew and Tanith are my own (now adult) son and daughter and they have given permission for me to quote from the informal diaries I kept of their first five years.